LIGHT IN THE VALLEY

The McCurdy Mission School Story

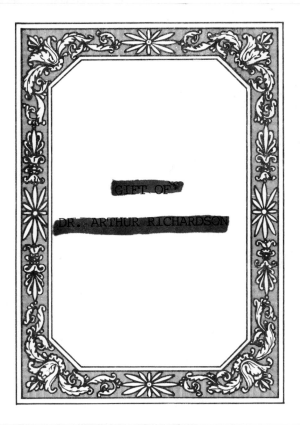

The founder, Miss Mellie Perkins, about 1915.

LIGHT IN THE VALLEY
The McCurdy Mission School Story

Robert H. Terry

90-205

Sunstone Press
Santa Fe, New Mexico

THIRD PRINTING
Printed in the United States of America

Library of Congress Cataloging in Publication Data:

Terry, Robert H. 1935-
   Light in the valley.

   Bibliography: p. 141.
   Includes index.
   1. McCurdy Mission School — History. 2. Methodist Church — Missions — New Mexico
3. United Methodist Church (U.S.) — Missions — New Mexico I. Title.
LD7501.E625T47   1986   377'.6'0978952   84-50388
ISBN: 0-86534-051-X (softcover)
ISBN: 0-86534-053-6 (limited)

Published in 1987 by Sunstone Press / Post Office Box 2321 / Santa Fe, NM 87504-2321 USA

DEDICATION

*To the faculty, staff and students
of The McCurdy Mission School —
past, present and future.*

SCHOOL MOTTO
*"And Jesus increased in wisdom and stature,
and in favor with God and man."*   Luke 2:52

CONTENTS

Acknowledgements 9

Introduction 11

New Mexico:
      The Land, The People and Their Education 12

The Mission Begins:
      Pioneers, Preachers and Missionaries 24

The Mission Reaches Out 40

The McCracken Era 60

The Mission Expands and Faces the Future 102

Important Dates and Events in the History of
      The McCurdy Mission Schools 131

Pastors and McCurdy Mission School Workers 134

Bibliography 141

Index 145

ACKNOWLEDGEMENTS

Probably no historian has ever written a book alone, and this small volume is no exception. Many friends and colleagues have aided and advised in many ways, and I am indebted to them all. Some deserve special recognition and they are as follows: to York College of Pennsylvania, especially President and Mrs. Robert V. Iosue, Dean William A. DeMeester and Dr. Chin H. Suk, thank you for time, funds and encouragements; to Professors Elmer O'Brien and Shomy Eichenaur of The United Theological Seminary Library in Dayton, Ohio, for assistance in many ways; to Professor William C. Beal of The United Methodist Archives in Madison, New Jersey, who located lost material; to Audrey Brubaker for typing and friendship; to Jean Adair Eckert for timely and helpful suggestions; to Rev. Frank Bergstrom for field trips to various archives and for encouragement.

In New Mexico at The McCurdy Mission School the list of those who helped is endless. Special appreciation goes to Irene Cole for limitless aid; to David and Carol Burgett who suffered through the entire project with aid and good humor; to Dolph Pringle for his priceless insight into New Mexico; to Dale Robinson who introduced me to "green chile;" to Jim and Kathy Hemsworth who helped with the early stages; to Rev. Roger and Sandy Decker who escaped to St. Martin; to Rev. and Mrs. Elliot Graves, also to Rev. Dennis and DeeDee Heffner; to Will and Beth Hyde, Avis Williams, Bob and Yvonne Wood, Ruth and Pauline Stambach, Ken and Marian Martinez, James Thompson, and the many other friends and staff of The McCurdy School who have taken us into their homes and hearts. And to James C. Smith and the staff of Sunstone Press for their many kindly suggestions.

A special acknowledgement goes to my wife, Shirley, who has endured almost everything during this project and has done so with a smile.

Naturally, like all authors, the errors and mistakes are mine and mine alone, and when you spot them, please let me know. We shall both be wiser for the knowledge.

Robert H. Terry

INTRODUCTION

Light in the Valley is the historical story of The McCurdy Mission School in Española, New Mexico. Located in a region of great scenic beauty, the area suffers from high unemployment and chronic depression. Throughout the decades, education was much neglected in Northern New Mexico. Responding to the need for educational opportunity, Miss Mellie Perkins opened the first small mission school in Velarde in 1912.

From the opening day of the boarding school, McCurdy Mission has served as a home away from home for literally hundreds of students. From the first graduating class of six students in 1926, the school has grown to a 44-acre campus with an enrollment of over 500 students in grades one through twelve.

Farming programs, athletics, community recreation programs, new church congregations, elementary schools, a community hospital and a nursing program have all been outreaches of this Christian mission. Indeed the deep faith and Christian commitment of the dedicated faculty and staff through the years have served to make this a truly special school.

Outside of New Mexico the United Methodist Church as a whole has never really heard the full story of The McCurdy Mission. Long neglected has been the historical drama of this remarkable school where so many people have given so much to improve the lives of others with little or no thought of personal gain or recognition. Through the pages of *Light in the Valley* church members and other interested people will learn the full story of the Christian love, influence and dedication of The McCurdy Mission School.

NEW MEXICO

The Land, The People and Their Education

New Mexico has been called "The Land of Sunshine," but periodically huge black thunderheads do roll across the state bringing some much needed rain. New Mexico has also been called "The Land of Adobe;" however, today high-rise office buildings pierce the sky in cities like Albuquerque. Writers have also referred to New Mexico as "The Land of Silence," but today jet planes break the sound barrier at airbases like Cannon, Holloman and Kirtland while missiles at White Sands regularly smash the desert silence. More recently New Mexico is being called "The Land of Enchantment" and that it is, for the land forms, climate and people are remarkable in their variety. In fact, six of the world's known life zones exist within the state's 121,412 square miles.

Geographically, New Mexico is a state of remarkable diversity. From lofty pine covered mountains in the north and west, including the southern ranges of the Rockies, to the cactus-covered deserts of the south; from the buffalo plains (llano estacado or staked plain) in the east to the mesas of "Indian Country" in the west, elevations vary from a low of 2,842 feet at the Pecos River near Carlsbad to over 13,000 feet on Wheeler Peak near Taos.

High, dry and relatively unpolluted, the brisk air of high altitudes combined with the low humidity of the Southwest and virtually year-round sunshine combine to make New Mexico someplace special. To this add majestic mountains like the Sangre de Cristo (Blood of Christ); plants like the yucca, chamisa, sage, juniper, piñon and cactus; include chile patches, fruit orchards, the Rio Grande, topped off with a deep turquoise colored sky and New Mexico is indeed a "Land of Enchantment."

Explaining the magic of New Mexico to a person who has never been there is difficult, and perhaps it is best described in the words of Pulitzer Prize winner Oliver LaFarge:

> It is a vast, harsh, poverty-stricken, varied and beautiful land, a breeder of artists and warriors. It is home, by birth or passionate adoption, of a wildly assorted population which has shown itself capable of achieving homogeneity without sacrificing its diversity. It is primitive, undeveloped, overused, new, raw, rich with tradition, old and mellow. It is a land full of the essence of peace, although its history is one of invasions and conflicts. It is itself, an entity, at times infuriating, at times utterly delightful to its lovers, a land that draws and holds men and women with ties

that cannot be explained or submitted to reason.[1]

The river bottoms, game rich plains and protected mountain valleys of this enchanting land have attracted and sustained man since at least 12,000 B.C. Sandia Cave near Albuquerque is the location of the earliest known archaeological site in the entire Southwest. Folsom Man, whose stone darts were uncovered along with the remains of post-glacial bison on the eastern plains near Raton and the occupants of Bat Cave who left remnants of domestic maize out on the San Augustin Plains were the other prehistoric residents of the area.[2]

Indian farmers located in places like the Mesa Verde (now a National Park in southwest Colorado), Aztec, Bandelier and Chaco Canyon (National Monuments) in western New Mexico were the original inhabitants of the area. These pre-Columbian people had a highly developed religion, created lasting villages, worked in pottery and weaving and built sophisticated road and irrigation systems. Experts now believe that these Indians traded with such far away places as Mexico and the Pacific coast. By the time that Francisco Vasquez de Coronado and his Spanish conquistadores marched into New Mexico (New Spain) in 1540, drought and hostile marauders had forced the early Indians into scattered pueblos (so named because they resembled Spanish towns.)

As Herbert Eugene Bolton writes in his epic story of the expedition:
> Coronado and his men saw and described on the basis of eye-witness information the Zuni Pueblos, the Hopi Pueblos, Colorado River and the Giant Yuman tribes along the River of the Firebrands. Farther east they were the first to see Acoma, "the Sky City," the upper Rio Grande, the Tiquex Pueblos along its banks, snow-covered Sangre de Cristo Mountains, Pecos River, Canadian River, the vast herds of buffaloes, and the great canyons of the Staked Plains, as later they were miscalled by the Anglo-American pioneers. They first explored the Texas Panhandle, first crossed Oklahoma, the Cimarron and Arkansas rivers, traversed eastern Kansas and became acquainted with the tatooed Wichitas. These helmet-crested Spanish horsemen saw and made known to the world most of the places visited today by myriad travelers in the region now known in the United States as the Far Southwest.[3]

In 1598 under the leadership of Don Juan de Oñate the first permanent European settlers to New Mexico came north from Mexico.

Accompanying him on this thousand mile trip which took two years were ten Franciscan padres, and one hundred twenty-nine soldier-colonists and their families. Oñate's encampment was at first called San Juan de los Caballeros (near the present site of the San Juan Pueblo north of Española). Later this camp was moved west across the Rio Grande and renamed San Gabriel de los Españoles. To the local Indians the site is still known as Yungue yungue, and gradually the Spanish name was shortened to merely Española. The present town is a short drive from the original location. At the time of its settlement, San Gabriel was a thousand miles from any other European community.

Great is the drama of these early years, and many fascinating stories of northern New Mexico await the patient work of scholars. For example, the Oñate expedition brought some 3,000 sheep, 1,000 goats, 300 black cattle and 150 mares and colts. Today only the Navajo have this unique "churro" strain of sheep. What makes this intriguing is that the now-famous weaving tradition of mountain villages like Chimayo has its roots in these curious animals. Indeed the chief source of revenue to the Spanish settlers in the early days was the flocks of the "Rio Arriba Country."

Knowledgeable area historians also maintain that the story of young Cristobal Oñate is a legend of its own. Son of the great Spanish captain, Cristobal was only ten years old on the Jornada del Muerte (Journey of Death) that brought the Spanish north. When he was only thirteen he was with the explorers out on the Great Plains. By the age of sixteen he was acting governor while his father journeyed to the Pacific coast. At the age of twenty by election of his own associates, most of whom were much older, Cristobal was chosen to succeed his father as governor. He remained in command until the arrival of Governor Peralta in 1609.

Hardships, quarrels, lack of rich mines and finally wholesale desertion of the northern-most colony in the Spanish Empire finally forced the re-location in 1610 (ten years before the landing at Plymouth Rock) down river to Santa Fe.

Following the change of command at Santa Fe, the Oñates started for their old home deep in Mexico. "Somewhere between the Española Valley and El Paso the party was surprised by a savage horde of Indians and Cristobal was killed. He fills an unknown grave in the state his father founded."[4]

15

For thousands of years before the coming of the Spanish, the Indians of the Rio Grande Valley had lived in relative peace with each other. During the decades of Spanish rule, the Pueblo Indians suffered many indignities. Frequently they were forced to work in the fields, mines and sweatshops and at times were little more than slaves. As the number and size of the Spanish settlements grew, the Franciscan padres worked to convert the Indians to Christianity. For many, this was the worst insult of all. They were being forced to exchange their ancient religious customs into those of the Spanish. Outwardly conforming but inwardly seething, the two cultures ultimately clashed.

In 1675 a medicine man from the San Juan Pueblo named Pope emerged as a powerful leader. Plans were carefully laid and by August 1680, the Pueblo Revolt was in motion across northern New Mexico. Thousands of Pueblo Indians (est. 20,000) participated in an attempt to overthrow the Spanish. "The settlers in the Española Valley in some cases made their way to Santa Cruz and fortified that village. They sent word of their plight to Governor Otermin in Santa Fe who sent reinforcements which rescued the colonists and conducted them to the capital."[5]

Santa Fe was surrounded and cut off from its water supply. Parts of the town were occupied and destroyed. Governor Otermin and the colnists fought their way out of town and "...on Monday, August 21, 1680 a thousand frightened people made ready to start south."[6] The forced retreat took them all the way to El Paso. The Indians never attacked; for them the Spaniards leaving was victory enough.

Some 2,500 Spanish colonists were killed in the struggle. Priests were frequently singled out for brutal deaths. At least twenty-one priests died during the revolt.

Pope and his followers tried to restore the old ways. Christian baptism was to be removed and use of the Spanish language was forbidden. Christian marriages were annulled. Churches were burned or dismantled. All Christian books and documents were burned. Even the fruit trees were dug up and the domestic animals killed. As a result, very little is known of the thirteen years of Indian occupation in Santa Fe. Historians do know a drought lasted some seven years and that most of the Indians were close to starvation.

Don Diego de Vargas (the rest of his name is Zapata y Lujan Ponce de Leon) who had kept the New Mexican colonists together in El Paso returned to Santa Fe on September 13, 1692, and received the Indian surrender without a shot being fired. Peace throughout the region was not so easy to attain and, for the next three years at least sporadically, the fighting continued (Today the Spanish reconquest is commemorated—at least by the Spanish—each fall in the Santa Fe Fiesta.)

The Española Valley relates to the "re-entrada" in two unique ways. For one thing the head man of all the Pueblo Indians at the time was a San Juan Indian named Luis Tapatu. It was to this man that de Vargas sent his own rosary and asked for peace. Without the moral and military assistance of this man, the reconquest would not have been so easy or so peaceful. Secondly, in April of 1695, de Vargas personally led settlers back into Santa Cruz. The local Indians who had walled and occupied Santa Cruz were told to move to Chimayo and San Juan. With the resettlement of the valley, the village was named La Villa Nueva de Santa Cruz de los Españoles Mexicanos del rey Nuestro Don Carlos Segundo.[7]

For 150 years New Mexico served as the northern-most outpost of Spain in the New World. In 1821 it became a part of the Republic of Mexico. Life was always difficult, and "Mother Mexico" was linked only by the Camino Real (Chihuahua Trail) which ran 450 miles from Santa Fe to Chihuahua. In spite of raids by the Apaches, Navajos, Utes and Comanches, the region grew. New villages were founded, ranches developed and mission churches built.

Following Mexican independence New Mexico was open to trade with the United States. Prior to this time traders coming down the Santa Fe Trail, as the link to the United States was called, risked the fate of Zeb Pike who in 1806 was sent to Chihuahua in chains. By 1821 William Becknell had opened the Santa Fe Trail all the way from Missouri and trading flourished. Santa Fe became the way to go to California and New Mexico was opened up to American trade, influence and settlement.

When General Stephen Kearny raised the American flag over the Palace of the Governors in Santa Fe in 1846, New Mexico became a United States territory. The action in Santa Fe was without resistance; however, in Taos the Mexican uprising the next year killed the territorial Governor, Charles Bent.

Official American title to New Mexico was concluded by the Treaty of Guadalupe Hidalgo which ended the War with Mexico. In 1853 parts of New Mexico and Arizona were added to the United States by the Gadsden Purchase.

During the Civil War, Texan Confederates moved up the Rio Grande Valley and captured Santa Fe in 1862. Union forces won at the battle of Glorieta Pass, located between Santa Fe and Las Vegas and thus probably preserved both the gold fields of Colorado and California for the Union.

It has been said that in the half century following the Civil War, the New Mexican territory lived up to the image of the "Wild West." Indian wars were fought against the Apaches, Navajos and Utes. Kit Carson, famous frontiersman from Taos, carried out these expeditions until the Indians accepted reservations (Geronimo quit fighting in 1886). Range wars scarred the territory. The most famous were the Colfax County War and Lincoln County War of the 1870s. Billy the Kid became a sort of celebrity as a result of these struggles.

Mining hit New Mexico in the 1870s. Boom towns opened all over the state. Gold, silver, copper, lead, zinc and turquoise boomed and busted leaving the state dotted with ghost towns. In the 20th century, mining has become big business with coal first, then oil and gas, and finally uranium.

Railroads reached Albuquerque in 1880 closing the old Santa Fe Trail. (At Fort Union one can still see the wagon ruts.) Even though a certain railroad line was named for Santa Fe, the railroad never reached the capital city — and it still hasn't. As a result, Albuquerque rapidly outgrew Santa Fe as the state's economic center. Finally in 1912 after numerous attempts, New Mexico was admitted to the Union as the 47th state.

Immigration which was rapid to the entire West following the Civil War has only produced a permanent population today (1980) of 1,303,000 people. (The cities of Philadelphia and Phoenix are larger.) This represents a current density pattern of just ten people per square mile and there is good evidence that there are more cattle than people within the state. However, change is once again occurring, for the decade of the 1970s the New Mexico rate of growth of 19.2% was nearly three times that of the national average. As the Sunbelt grows so does New Mexico, but at present, it retains its distinctly rural character. More importantly, it has maintained its multicultural heritage. Anglos, Spanish, Apaches, Navajos, Pueblo Indians[8] and many other ethnic groups have blended to create a

18

unique culture. Indeed the "Land of Enchantment" has always been a very special place for art, architecture, dances, dress, feasts, fiestas, foods and lifestyles. Unfortunately for the people, the education available to them down through the years has not been very distinctive nor has it been readily available. Indeed until the coming of the 20th century New Mexico languished in the backwaters of academic achievement.

The history of education in New Mexico begins with the Franciscan missionaries, Fray Luis de Escalona and Fray Juan de Padilla. These teachers accompanied Coronado on his expedition to New Mexico in 1540. Both teachers stayed on after the soldiers had departed with Fray Padilla at Quivira and Fray de Escalona at Cicuye. Both men were murdered within two years. More Franciscans came with the Oñate expedition and reportedly tried to start schools along the Rio Grande in 1599. Father Benavides made a report to the King of Spain in 1630 in which he stated that industrial schools and shops had been established in each Pueblo. When the Spaniards were driven out in 1680, the schools along with the churches were destroyed. Today throughout New Mexico stand silent witnesses in the form of ancient adobe walls of these long abandoned early missions. By decrees of the King in 1721, public schools were to be established in the pueblos and in all of the Spanish settlements. In spite of this decree, education remained in a backward condition throughout the 18th century.

At the beginning of the 19th century, there really was not an educational institution worthy of the name. Santa Fe did have a private school in which the rudiments of Spanish grammar, Latin and philosophy were taught. The present day weaving of the Chimayo Valley north of Santa Fe started in 1805 when Ignacio and Juan Bozan were sent from Mexico to teach the art.[9] The best known school of the time was located at Taos, and it was the teacher of this school, Padre Martínez, who printed the first books in New Mexico. These were textbooks for his elementary pupils.[10]

The first school law under the rule of Mexico came on April 27, 1822. It provided that each town council was to form a primary public school. The results were basically negligible although a high school was started in El Paso in 1823. Virtually all repeated attempts to establish public schools prior to 1846 ended in defeat due to the lack of revenue. So little had happened in education that Governor Vigil in 1847 reported to the first New Mexico legislature that there was just one public school in the territory. This was located at Santa Fe and had only enough funds to hire one teacher.[11]

The most admirable attempt to improve education was made by Santa Fe's first Archbishop, Jean B. Lamy. During the 1850s, he established Loretto Academy for girls and St. Michael's College for boys in Santa Fe, and a Jesuit College in Las Vegas which was later moved to Colorado. Later at the Archbishop's urging small schools were started at Taos, Mora, Las Cruces, Bernalillo and a few other places. As might be expected in a predominantly Spanish territory, until the close of the Mexican War in 1848, Catholic missionaries were the only people interested in New Mexico and its education.

The American occupation brought Protestant missionaries to New Mexico for the first time. The Baptists were the first to enter in 1848, one year after the territory had been acquired from Mexico. They opened an English school that year and a school for boys and girls in 1849. The Presbyterian boards of home and foreign missions carried out extensive work between 1866 and 1878. Rev. John Menaul's school at Laguna was one of the most successful. In Santa Fe the first organized Spanish evangelical missionary work was started in 1867. Miss Charity Ann Gaston started a school in rented property that had been abandoned by the Baptists. In time this work became the famous Allison-James School.[12]

In the ten years from 1868 to 1878 Methodism was established in New Mexico. Rev. E.G. Nicholson was one of the earliest missionaries but permanent success came only when Rev. Thomas Harwood began his work. In 1871 he opened a mission school at Watrous in Eastern New Mexico. Rev. Harwood published the official newspaper of the Methodist Church in Santa Fe in both English and Spanish, and the influence of the Harwood Industrial School lasted many years.

The Congregationalists began their work in New Mexico in 1880. They soon had churches in Albuquerque and Santa Fe and established the Rio Grande Industrial School. For several years the Albuquerque Academy was supported by the Congregational Church. Northern Baptists had begun work north of Santa Fe by 1895. In that year they established a mission at Rinconada, in 1897 they started a school at Velarde and sometime later one at Alcalde. Their efforts lasted about a dozen years, when the Southern Baptists encouraged them (for some unknown reason) to abandon their work among the Spanish-speaking people of New Mexico.[13]

Throughout New Mexico's colonial and territorial period education never had a very high priority. Due to existing conditions the region was absolutely helpless to provide for an adequate educational system. Distances were great, transportation was inadequate, most of the people were poor, communications were difficult at best and there was danger from unfriendly Indians. Additionally, Spanish families were opposed to public education both for tax reasons and for the belief in territorial days that the children would lose their family traditions in Anglo schools.

The general state of education was exposed by the first official statewide census taken in 1870. This revealed that 73.5% of the people over ten years of age could not read and that 87.5% of the total population could not write.[14] As late as 1889 a law was passed which either indicated that teachers were inferior in training or that through a mistake the word "school teacher" was inserted in the law. The law requiring teachers to read and write is as follows:

> That hereafter in this territory no person who cannot read and write sufficiently to keep his own record in either English or Spanish languages, shall be eligible to be elected or appointed to hold the office of school teacher, school director, school treasurer, etc.[15]

Educational statistics of any kind during these early days are discouraging. For example, in 1829 the whole territory of New Mexico had only eighteen schools and eighteen teachers. in 1875 there were reported to be in the entire territory only 138 schools with 147 teachers. Even the coming of statehood in 1912 did not improve the educational system to much extent. It appears that the majority of the people were uninterested in an improved school system, especially if they had to pay for it. The rich were not very interested in the education of the poor. Language problems, generations of illiteracy and the basic stand of the Roman Catholic Church hindered education. The lack of schools as well as the poor condition of those available was adequate proof of the lack of interest in education.[16]

Article XXI, Section 4 of the New Mexico Constitution (1912) provides for a state school system:

Provision shall be made for the establishment and maintenance
of a system of public schools which shall be open to all children
of the state and free from sectarian control, and said schools shall
be always conducted in English.[17]

This provision was demanded by the United States Congress, for
the legislators themselves had not been interested enough in education to
include it in the original draft. Prior to the passage of the State School
Equalization Fund, it is doubtful if public schools could have existed in
certain regions of the State (especially the northern area) had not the
Catholic nuns taught in them. In counties such as Mora, Taos and Rio Arriba, there were school districts that did not raise more than thirty dollars
a year in tax revenues. At the time of statehood the conditions of most of
the rural schools were "deplorable." Many of the buildings were unfit for
human occupancy, teachers were poorly qualified and terms were ir-
regular in length.[18] To say that New Mexico, especially the area north of
Santa Fe, was ripe for the founding of The McCurdy Mission School is
certainly an understatement.

NOTES

[1] Oliver LaFarge, "New Mexico," in *The Spell of New Mexico*, ed. Tony Hillerman (Albuquerque: UNM Press, 1978), p. 21.

[2] Petroglyphs can be located in many parts of the state.

[3] Hebert Eugene Bolton, *Coronado: Knight of Pueblos and Plains* (Albuquerque: UNM Press, 1949), preface.

[4] Clara D. True, *Facts About the Española Valley* (Española, NM: The Rio Grande Sun, 1972), p. 10.

[5] True, p. 14.

[6] Franklin Folsom, *Red Power on the Rio Grande* (Chicago: Follett Publishing Company, 1973), p. 118.

[7] Meaning the new village of Santa Cruz of the Mexican Spanish of our King Don Carlos II.

[8] The nineteen pueblos are, from north to south, Taos, Picuris, San Juan, Nambe, Santa Clara, Tesuque, San Ildefonso, Pecos, Jemez, Cochití, Santo Domingo, San Felipe, Zia, Santa Ana, Laguna, Acoma, Zuni, Sandia and Isleta.

[9] S.P. Nanninga, *The New Mexico School System* (Albuquerque: UNM Press, 1942), p. 4.

[10] Nanninga, p. 4. Copies of these early school books are today in the State Museum at Santa Fe.

[11] Nanninga, p. 6.

[12] Schools such as Allison-James, Menaul, Rio Grande Indian School and Harwood Industrial School are all unique stories of their own. For example, see *100 Years From Founding of Menaul School 1881-1981*, Menaul Historical Library, Albuquerque, New Mexico.

[13] C. Whitney, "Progress on the Home Field," *Woman's Evangel* (June 1913) p. 165.

[14] *In the Valley of the Rio Grande* (Dayton, OH: The Home Mission and Church Erection Society, 1943), p. 6.

[15] Nanninga, p. 17.

[16] Tom Wiley, *Public School Education in New Mexico* (Albuquerque: Division of Government Research, UNM, 1965), p. 24.

[17] Nanninga, p. 18.

[18] Wiley, p. 27.

THE
MISSION BEGINS
Pioneers, Preachers and Missionaries

In order to more fully appreciate the historical drama of The Mc-Curdy Mission School one must realize that the Homestead Act of 1862 opened millions of acres of unoccupied lands in the Southwest to settlers. But by the turn of the century Oklahoma and Texas were filling up and thus only Arizona and New Mexico were left. Railroads ran excursions at low rates and thousands came to investigate the new land. One such pioneer was Rev. Wannamaker, a Congregational minister from the east who traveled west for his health.[1]

This inspired Christian man started a village in eastern New Mexico called Amistad in 1906. By placing ads for immigrants in religious periodicals he soon attracted a variety of religious settlers including Methodists, Presbyterians and United Brethren. Soon after, a young United Brethren minister from Kansas who came to visit his parents was invited to Amistad and he opened a mission field in the area. This young man was Rev. Clarence Schlotterbeck, and he is perhaps one of the most unsung heroes of the mission work in the Southwest.[2]

Rev. Schlotterbeck was appointed by the Home Mission Board in Dayton, Ohio, as "United Brethren Mission Superintendent for the Southwest, to organize religious life in communities without churches or pastors in that area, and with authority to establish denominational churches."[3] This young minister traveled extensively throughout eastern New Mexico and the panhandles of Texas and Oklahoma. His efforts resulted in the formation of at least eight congregations and the establishment of what became known as the North Texas Conference.

The first session of this new conference was held at the Childress Schoolhouse northwest of Amistad, in Union County, New Mexico, on November 5, 1908.[4] At that time the North Texas Conference was formally organized by Bishop William Werkley of Kansas City. Rev. Schlotterbeck transferred from the Southwest Kansas Conference and was named Conference Superintendent. Rev. Mrs. Callie King (who was to serve later at McCurdy) from Optima of the Oklahoma Conference was named the secretary. In addition to church officials from Dayton, nine ministers were present: three from Oklahoma, two from Texas, and three from New Mexico. Churches represented included Clapham and Amistad in New Mexico, Optima and Floris in Oklahoma, and Middlewater in Texas. Rev. Robert Hillis of the Methodist Protestant Church who served as advisor was received into the new conference.[5] Among the subjects discussed at this historic meeting were the organizational work at Sedan, Willow Creek, Eva, Hartville and Lispscomb; the need for Sunday Schools in the new area; and the progress of temperance and prohibition.

It was at the Second Meeting of the North Texas Conference that the name Mellie Perkins first appeared. Listed in the minutes as representing Dumas, Texas, she was in charge of the Young People's Society and apparently was named Conference Deaconess.[6] By this time there were twelve organized churches with one hundred twenty-nine members. Rev. Schlotterbeck was re-elected Presiding Elder and was released from his duties at Amistad to reach further west. Churches were soon founded at Wagon Mound and in other areas as far south as Las Vegas.

In recalling this early history of the United Brethren in the eastern plains of New Mexico, it is interesting to note that one of the early homesteaders was Rev. George Brandstetter, a circuit-rider from western Iowa, Minnesota and South Dakota. Brandstetter was admitted into the North Texas Conference at the Second Meeting in 1909. He filed a homestead claim in the Amistad area as did his sons George and Albert. Rev. George Brandstetter was assigned churches at Cone, Sedan, Centerville and everything in between. His son, Rev. Albert L. Brandstetter, went on to a successful career in the ministry both in eastern New Mexico and in the Rio Grande Valley.

Spring of 1910 turned out to be a special occasion as Rev. A.L. Brandstetter tells the story:

> I was in the field sowing grain, when I saw Rev. Schlotterbeck ride up to the house on his little whistle-tailed bronco. The bulging saddle bags and bed roll on his pony caused me to assume that he was on his way somewhere. He said he was going across the Sangre de Cristos into the Rio Grande Valley. It was a difficult journey by horseback and he did not know how long he would be gone or what he would find there. It could be although it was doubtful that there were some United Brethren people living in the valley, lost from their church.[7]

Rev. Brandstetter relates that Schlotterbeck's journey was to last for practically three months, and the round trip was eventually to cover a distance of some 600 miles, much of it mountainous terrain. It took him over the famous Old Santa Fe Trail, through Glorieta Pass to Santa Fe itself, then up toward Española and the Rio Grande.[8]

As Schlotterbeck traveled through the upper Rio Grande Valley, he saw that it was Spanish-speaking territory and he was deeply concerned to find some Anglo people located there, without religious services available, and many Spanish people in need of the Gospel. These were known as a "lost people" who had been living in this remote area for over 300 years, forgotten and neglected, first by Spain, then by Mexico and finally by the United States government in the on-going of time and civilization.[9]

By late summer Rev. Schlotterbeck was back at Amistad. Calling friends and neighbors together he reported with enthusiasm his trip and his dream to evangelize the area. From this meeting came the initial gift of $1,000 from Mr. and Mrs. Richard Hauser to establish work at Velarde and the offer that Miss Mellie Perkins made to go to the Rio Grande Valley mission field.[10]

Immortalized among those individuals responsible for advancing the cause of education in northern New Mexico is Miss Mellie Perkins. Originally from Fort Wayne, Indiana, Miss Perkins served part of 1907 as a teacher in Colorado but severe illness, which was to plague her periodically throughout her entire life, caused her to return to Indiana. Upon recovery she came west again to visit a sister in the panhandle of Texas. Being of United Brethren background she soon accepted a position at Optima, Oklahoma, assisting Rev. Callie King. It was here that she met her first Spanish-Americans and became aware of their many needs.[11]

Following that historic meeting with Schlotterbeck in Amistad, Miss Perkins began to prepare herself for the new mission field. Thus she was not at the Third Conference Meeting held at Amistad in 1910 although there was a paper on Christian Stewardship written by her but read by another member. The Fourth Conference in September of 1911 reveals that "Miss Perkins read a splendid paper on Sunday Schools."[12]

During the school year 1911-1912, Miss Perkins temporarily left her work in the North Texas Conference in order to attend Campbell College in Holton, Kansas. Here she studied the Spanish language and otherwise prepared herself for the new mission work in New Mexico. It was at this time that she became friends with the young teacher Edith McCurdy.

On a previous visit to the Rio Grande Valley Miss Perkins had heard of the abandoned Baptist property at Velarde and had brought it to the attention of the Home Mission Board. While Miss Perkins was away at college the property was secured and the field was ready for the planting.

Miss Perkins tells the story best herself:

> I landed at Velarde October 12, 1912. I had stopped in Santa Fe and purchased just the necessary articles to start housekeeping with the money gathered in the East, which was less than $100, and had them shipped to Velarde. As we (I was taking a young lady from Wagon Mound) went along the D.&R.G. (known as the Chile Line) I must confess that things did not look very bright, and the nearer we came to our destination the drearier grew the scenes, and when we landed across the Rio Grande and found we had to walk the ties on the railroad bridge in order to cross, we felt quite uncomfortable, but I did not dare to show the white feather as I saw the tears in the eyes of my friend. However, we got across and found some American people in charge of the lumber yard who gave us assistance and took our baggage to the mission.[13]

She goes on to say:

> I must confess as I walked that mile to the mission and saw nothing but dark-faced Mexicans (Spanish-Americans) staring at me, I felt that I was in a country far from home and kindred and that my desires were fast vanishing but I called on One who gives strength and courage when needed most and my spirits soon rose. The mission property had been unused for four years, and you can draw some conclusion of its dilapidated appearance. We found the house had leaked and water-soaked up through the floors and these were heeved, and the walls were crumbling and it had a most sickening musty odor all through it. Our goods not having arrived we found lodging with a Spanish family for the night. Early the next morning we began cleaning and shoveling out the dirt and mud and when the goods came we proceeded to make three rooms habitable by means of store boxes and improvised furniture.[14]

Miss Perkins' only real companion that first year was Susanita Martinez, the young girl who had come to Velarde with her from Wagon Mound. During the months to come she reported that she cleaned up weeds, fixed broken fences, cleared fallen buildings, repaired the house in addition to the real mission. School had opened on October 21 with four pupils and ended in May with forty-three. A local Protestant Spanish-American girl named Rafaelita Garcia, who was a public school teacher, gave valuable assistance during the spring months.

In March the Rev. N.H. Huffman, who had just returned from Puerto Rico, came to the Española Valley to investigate the mission field and its prospects. He spent ten days conducting services and was firmly convinced of the great need of mission work in New Mexico. A special plea was sent to the Board to start work at Albuquerque because it had become a railroad center and 5,000 men were coming into the town for employment, but the request had to be denied for lack of funds.[15]

Apparently the closing exercises that first year were a very special occasion.

> We are planning for an entertainment for the last day. They enjoy the exercise and are all very anxious to take part, from the smallest to the largest desiring to recite (so different from our American boys). As they never have anything of this kind, only what the plaza schools furnish, we enjoy the preparation also, although more work and worry than the every-day school work would be. We do not take much time from the school work for this though, but take outside hours for practice. I think we shall spend the day picnicking in the mountains or along the river, and then have our exercises in the evening.[16]

Miss Perkins felt that the first year was successful but noted, "...next year the school work will be much heavier, and I am hoping and praying some persons will be inclined to answer the call and give themselves to this work. To me, the work is delightful and the blessings received from real service more than repay."[17]

In his annual report for 1912 Dr. C. Whitney notes:

> Miss Mellie Perkins is throwing her life into this mission, conducting day-school, preaching, superintending Sunday school, acting as physician, burying their dead and otherwise making herself a necessity to that community.[18]

At the Sixth Annual Meeting, which was the final session, of the North Texas Conference held at Optima, Oklahoma, in 1913, Miss Perkins gave the first report on the Spanish School at Velarde. It was at this meeting that the decision was made to terminate the Conference. The churches at Eva, Floris and Optima went back to Oklahoma while the churches at Amistad, Cone, Onava, Santa Fe, Sedan, Velarde and Wagon Mound became the New Mexico Conference.

The happenings of the 1913-1914 school year at Velarde are almost unknown except for the fact that Miss Bessie Haffner of Illinois answered the call to the mission field. Records indicate that she worked at Velarde until 1916. A further advance was made by the locating of Rev. Nicholas Huffman in Santa Fe. During January of 1914 he and Elder Schlotterbeck conducted services in Santa Fe, at the San Ildefonso Pueblo, at a home in Santa Cruz and at the mission in Velarde.[19] This proved to be a valuable church link in the upper Rio Grande Valley.

The arrival and help of Miss Haffner enabled Miss Perkins to answer an appeal from a group of Anglos at Santa Cruz, some sixteen miles down the Rio. With the close of school at Velarde in the spring of 1915, Miss Perkins and a young girl named Angelica Romero moved to Santa Cruz. School opened for eight students on October 11, 1915, in a small adobe house called the Borrego building. This structure was situated on McCurdy Road and was torn down in 1962.

> By the aid of subscriptions secured from the Board meeting at York, Nebraska and from other sources, two and a half acres of ground were purchased. On this there now stands a fine two-story adobe building—part of the building is used for school purposes and the rest for living and rooming.[20]

As has been previously mentioned, Miss Perkins had spent a year at Campbell College in Holton, Kansas, preparing for her work at Velarde. Part of her time was spent studying the Spanish language under the direction of Miss Edith McCurdy who was an instructor of Spanish and Oratory at the college.

Miss McCurdy was a very beautiful young lady from an affluent family in Lebanon County, Pennsylvania. The McCurdy family was very well educated; her father was a lawyer and her mother a teacher, and they were devoutly United Brethren. This recent Wellesley College graduate had gone to Kansas for her first year of teaching. She and Miss Perkins became friends and during the following year Edith McCurdy wrote encouraging letters and sent money for the mission work. During the summer of 1912 this young teacher traveled home to Pennsylvania, became ill and died quite unexpectedly. Her grieving father gave a thousand dollars in her memory to the Santa Cruz Mission. The first mission building was dedicated in November 1915 by Bishop Kephart and Superintendent

Huffman and was named The Edith M. McCurdy Mission.[21]

Aid and assistance for Miss Perkins came first in the form of Mary Brawner. Born in Danville, Illinois, she was converted at the age of twelve in a Methodist Church. During her high school years she attended a small United Brethren Mission Church. She relates that during an Annual Conference of her junior year

> ...it seemed that the Lord came and sat beside me in the pew and began talking to me about being a missionary for him. I can remember no part of the service itself. It seemed there was only the Lord and me there.[22]

Following high school she attended Bonebrake Seminary. After being ordained a deaconess she arrived in Santa Cruz. She was in charge of the work at Velarde from 1916 to 1925 and was assisted with her work there by Miss Irma Moore.

During this time it was necessary to build a mission house at Velarde to accommodate the increased enrollment. A chapel was also started but due to the increase in prices because of American entering World War I, neither the Board nor the local members could finish it for some time.

During the summer of 1916 Miss Perkins left the mission to attend to a sister who was ill in Texas. She shared her feelings on return:

> As usual, our train was nearly two hours late but I found Miss Brawner and some friends at the station to meet me...I was so tired that I felt I must have a week in which to rest, but nothing so fortunate for me. Miss Brawner had to go to Velarde to look after our interests there and keep the work going, so that left me alone again this summer to do the mission work, house and superintend the completion of the house and erection of the chapel. Cherries were ripe and had to be cared for, sick and other calls to make, plans for getting material and workmen for the building to be attended to, and the trip to Velarde to be made. This was the "rest" for the first week.[23]

Additional teaching help in the form of Miss Lillian Kendig arrived on September 2, 1916. Born and brought up in Franklin County, Pennsylvania, her father was both a church trustee and a Sunday School Superintendent. Educated in the public schools, she received a teacher's certificate from the State Normal School (2 years), spent one six week term at Lebanon Valley College and transferred to Bonebrake Seminary. Here she was graduated with honors in 1913.[24]

She too had felt the call of the Lord: "In 1913, I was teaching school in Pennsylvania when I felt the Lord calling me to some definite service for Him."[25] Like many of the early missionaries she vividly remembered her first impressions of the area:

> I'll never forget the narrow gauge D.&R.G. [Denver and Rio Grande] railroad that took us through the most wonderful lofty mountains nor the Indians on the platform of the station trying to sell pottery nor the two horse wagon that took us over the narrow sandy road through the Santa Cruz plaza to the mission building.[26]

Fall of 1916 found Miss Perkins acting as superindendent, directing the building of the chapel and directing the school and work at Velarde. In the midst of this activity she suffered a severe gallstone attack and was rushed to the hospital in Albuquerque for an operation. The new girls' matron (by now there were eight girls in the boarding school), Mrs. Lillian Markey, accompanied Miss Perkins to the hospital. Thus the opening of school was left to Miss Brawner and the new Miss Leila Luckey at Velarde, and to Miss Kendig and Miss Martinez at Santa Cruz.

A word about Miss Susanita Martinez is in order at this point for she was the pride and joy of the mission. Originally she had accompanied Miss Perkins from Wagon Mound on the first trip. She had gone on through the eight grades at Velarde thus becoming the first Spanish pupil in Rio Arriba County to receive a diploma. She received a scholarship to the Presbyterian School Allison-James in Santa Fe (a two year school at the time) and then was graduated from Santa Fe High School. After becoming the first Spanish-American deaconess, she was appointed to Santa Cruz.[27] Miss Martinez married a Methodist minister and left the mission school at the close of the school year.

Many were the hardships of these early mission school teachers. The poverty and general isolation were bad enough, but the constant opposition of the priests against a new religion in their area made life almost intolerable. It was no small task to win a convert in the beginning of mission work in New Mexico. Many who were attracted to the Protestant schools were hindered by the fear of physical violence or the effect of social pressure or of actually being cast out by their families. As one publication has put it:

> The church at large has never known the story of the persecution and sacrifice endured by the missionaries in these areas. There were hardships and privations not surpassed on any foreign field.[28]

Mary Brawner reported that "There was considerable opposition during the first years at Velarde as there was throughout the valley—during one severe wave of opposition Bibles and religious Protestant literature—along with school books were burned publicly in several plazas throughout the valley."[29] It seems that Santa Cruz fared even worse:

> The priest required all the people to bring their Bibles and other books including those distributed by our missionaries for examination. These were piled in the church yard and burned. One of the boys from our school snatched from the burning embers a copy of "Children's Stories of the New Testament" in Spanish. For years it appeared that this book was in the library of the Home Mission Society as a symbol that the Bible was a forbidden book and needed to be opened to the people.[30]

As fate would have it one of the young men who assisted the priest in the Bible burning at Velarde became converted some years later.

> Fidel Gutierrez—became evidence to the mission workers and church people that the Lord continues to bless even after persecution...While selling fruits and chile up country he was converted while staying in the home of one of his customers. He wrote to the mission teachers saying he was bringing his family to join the church the following Sunday. Long in the memories of those joyous teachers were the Christian smiles and testimony of this man who had come to know the Lord.[31]

Bible burning certainly was not the only trouble during the 1916-1917 school year. In January, Mrs. Markey, from Otterbein Memorial Church in Baltimore, Maryland, girls' matron, was hospitalized and was unable to return to work. She was to be greatly missed as she had been especially capable at performing social work. Miss Perkins was also hospitalized for a short time again.

The mission work seemed to be developing quite substantially and in August 1916 the first pastoral assignment was made. At the Third Annual Session of the North Texas Conference held in Wagon Mound on August 24, 1916, the Rev. T.Z. Salazar, the first local Spanish-American United Brethren pastor was appointed to the work at Santa Cruz and Velarde.

According to early records Rev. Salazar was born of Spanish Catholic parents in Los Pinos, New Mexico, and received a Catholic education. In 1894 he was converted during a revival at a mission school at Dulce, New Mexico. He was recruited to the ministry in 1901 in Dulce by a certain Mrs. T. Harwood. After studying at Albuquerque College, he was appointed in 1902 as assistant pastor there, studying and preaching until 1905. From then until his appointment in 1916 he had been working at various locations in Colorado and New Mexico.

Miss Perkins wrote this of him:

> Mr. Salazar has been recommended as a conscientious Christian whose soul is burdened for the salvation of his race. Thus far we have found him to be all that he is recommended, and more, too —good speaker, good preacher, and always ready to testify for his Master. His family, consisting of wife and four children, we consider a great credit to our work, and a splendid addition to the United Brethren mission family at Velarde.[32]

We know very little of him after his appointment except that he conducted evening services at Velarde and helped to lay the cornerstone of the new chapel. Regarding his dismissal Miss Kendig says, "Miss Perkins thought our facilities were not good enough and his services were discontinued."[33]

Rev. Richard Campbell, author of *Los Conquistadores*, writes:

> Local residents either have no memory of him at all or remember that he was here without any recollection of his departure. The gentleman seems to have vanished from sight and memory. It is the great unsolved mystery of Santa Cruz Church.[34]

The beginnings of the mission work at Alcalde, located midway between Santa Cruz and Velarde, are a special story of their own. As related through the words of an early issue of the *Woman's Evangel*, it appears that Miss Perkins was passing through the town when she was approached by Mr. Clark, one of the leading citizens, who urged her to open a school at Alcalde. The citizens had made an offer of free land, free adobe and help with hauling and construction. When asked by Miss Perkins why they were so anxious to have such a school, Mr. Clark replied that the work at Velarde and Santa Cruz missions had shown to them the importance of enlightenment and education.[35]

According to the story, when the local boys went to work for the mines and railroads in Colorado, the mission school boys received ten to fifty percent higher wages because "...they are more faithful and do their work better, and can understand English."[36] The economic side of an education was hitting home, and local parents were determined to have a school for their children.

Work at the Alcalde school started on July 1, 1917, under the direction of Miss Shanklin, a former missionary to Africa and the special representative of the Christian Endeavor societies of the East Ohio Branch. Miss Shanklin conducted industrial work during the summer of 1917 for both the boys and girls and opened the school in September.

While the new school building was under construction, Miss Perkins wrote:

> We have rented a typical Mexican house, very comfortable but not so nice looking. The schoolroom is thirty by fifteen, and the living room fourteen and one-half by sixteen. A shed room will be built on for fuel and storeroom.[37]

Even the "going" to Velarde must have been something to see for as Mellie Perkins tells it,

> ...I got a team and wagon of a neighbor and loaded in all that was left. The seat was too small for three of us, so Lillian (Kendig) got two cushions and sat in the table that was turned upside-down in the rear end. Miss Shanklin and I occupied the spring seat, of course I had to in order to drive.[38]

Apparently Miss Perkins' many talents also included being a wagonmaster.

It becomes difficult to keep account of the various teachers who came and went from each of the schools. Some stayed but a few months and others for years. School records reveal that Miss Bessie Haffner served at Velarde from 1913-1916. Miss Leila Luckey served first at Velarde in 1916-1917 and then at Alcalde in 1918-1919. Miss Anna Hardy was at Velarde from 1918 to 1922 and Miss Irma Moore served 1915-1916. Miss Shanklin, previously mentioned, arrived in June 1917 and left at the end of school 1918. Dr. Zonora Griggs served five months at Alcalde, and Miss Bertha Wolheiter taught at both Alcalde and Velarde from 1918 to 1924. Miss Lula Clippinger arrived on the mission field in March 1920 and remained at Alcalde for over a decade before transferring to Vallecitos.

Attendance at each school varied from term to term. The monthly reports for 1917 from the mission teachers show an attendance at Velarde of fifty-four and twenty-seven at Santa Cruz.[39]

Sunday, September 2, 1917, was the formal dedication of the new chapel at Santa Cruz. Dr. P.M. Camp officiated and Mr. and Mrs. E.E. McCurdy were present, having traveled all the way from Lebanon, Pennsylvania. Dr. Camp described the chapel:

> The chapel and school is a most magnificent two-story building, made of sun-burned brick and stuccoed, making it a most beautiful finish. In the basement story are two commodious, splendidly lighted and well-furnished modern schoolrooms. Upstairs is a most convenient auditorium, with small lecture rooms and pastor's study, that will seat 250-300 people. The furnace in the chapel is not yet put in, but is on the ground. The lawn will need grading yet to complete the work.
>
> As it stands the entire cost of both buildings, furnishings, out buildings, ground, everything, cost a little less than $8,000...[40]

Miss Kendig remembers that special day:

> Miss Perkins and I went to the altar to receive the keys of our new house of worship. What a responsibility, we dedicated our lives anew to his service. A church organization was effected and the charter members were Mellie Perkins, Lillian Kendig, Esther Peterson, Mary Brawner, Helica Romero and Fidel Roybal.[41]

Throughout the fall and winter of 1917-1918 Miss Perkins was ill frequently. Miss Lottie Newman from Willard, Ohio, came, apparently to visit, and remained some months filling in at a variety of jobs without pay. In the spring. Rev. Callie King, one of the original members of the North Texas Conference (the handwritten records of the first session in 1908 bear her name), came to hold Easter services. She stayed on through the summer working at the school and with various pastoral duties. Due to the illness of her aged mother she left the area in August 1918.

When Miss Kendig returned east to Pennsylvania for a rest in the summer of 1918, little did she dream of the changes that were about to take place. Accompanying her on the summer vacation was sixteen-year-old Manuelita Martinez from the Santa Cruz School. She attended summer school while Miss Kendig attended Branch and Board Meetings.

Miss Perkins left in June for a month's vacation. However, by July she had traveled to her sick mother in Graybill, Indiana. For reasons unknown but probably due to her own illnesses as well as her mother's she abruptly resigned from the mission field, thus ending an era. She had arrived on the scene in the Southwest a decade before, had worked in the old North Texas Conference and in six years had established three schools in the Valley of the Rio Grande.

Rev. Richard Campbell tells us that once back in Indiana, Miss Perkins worked for awhile in the local welfare department and then as the matron of a W.C.T.U. home for girls. Again her ill health forced her to give up her job. She moved to Bakersfield, California, tried teaching again, but died on June 15, 1924, in Puente, California.[42]

Miss Kendig wrote this tribute:

> In loving memory of Miss Mellie E. Perkins. There are many monuments built to the memory of great men and women, but the greatest monuments in the world are the deeds and influences of a great life. The three missions in the Rio Grande Valley for Spanish Americans shall forever stand in loving remembrance of the heroism, energy, and love of Miss Mellie Perkins.[43]

Perhaps Miss Perkins said it best herself:

> ...the seed has been sown, and we hope and pray some of it has fallen on good ground. Then Jesus says, "My word shall not return unto me void," so I sow in faith, believing and trusting in His promise.[44]

NOTES

[1] A.L. Brandstetter, *Mission Pioneering in New Mexico,* Unpublished Paper, October 1972, p. 2.

[2] Brandstetter, p. 3.

[3] Brandstetter, p. 4.

[4] Microfilm of the handwritten minutes of the North Texas Conference, United Theological Seminary, Dayton, Ohio.

[5] Microfilm of North Texas Conference.

[6] Microfilm of North Texas Conference. Proof of this is difficult to ascertain as five pages of the original notes are missing from the microfilm copy.

[7] Interview with Rev. Albert L. Brandstetter, Los Alamos, New Mexico, May 14, 1981.

[8] Interview with Brandstetter.

[9] Interview with Brandstetter.

[10] Interview with Brandstetter.

[11] Virginia Frank, Unpublished Papers, McCurdy Mission School Files, undated, p. 2.

[12] Microfilm of North Texas Conference.

[13] *Our Work in New Mexico,* Dayton, Ohio: The Home Mission and Church Erection Society, 1916, p. 13.

[14] *Our Work in New Mexico,* p. 13.

[15] *Our Work in New Mexico,* p. 13.

[16] Mellie Perkins, "Our School at Velarde," *Woman's Evangel* (May 1913), p. 134.

[17] Perkins, p. 135.

[18] Dr. C. Whitney, "Progress in the Home Field," *Woman's Evangel* (June 1913), p. 165.

[19] N.H. Huffman, "Just a Family Letter," *Woman's Evangel* (February 1914), p. 67.

[20] Ida A. Hushower, "Our Girls in New Mexico," *Woman's Evangel* (April 1916), p. 151.

[21] Interview with Mrs. Lily McCurdy Eakin, Mechanicsburg, Pennsylvania, April 1, 1982.

[22] Undated letter from Mary Brawner to McCurdy Mission believed to be for the 50th Anniversary in 1965.

[23] Mellie Perkins, "Back Again in New Mexico," *Woman's Evangel* (September 1916), p. 314.

[24] Rev. A.R. Clippinger, *Woman's Evangel* (September 1916), p. 304.

[25] Lillian Kendig Cole, *My Nine Years at McCurdy*, Unpublished Papers, McCurdy Mission, p. 1.

[26] Lillian Kendig Cole, p. 2.

[27] Mary E. Brawner, "After a Year in New Mexico," *Woman's Evangel* (October 1916), p. 339.

[28] In the Valley of the Rio Grande (Dayton, Ohio: The Home Mission and Church Erection Society, 1943), p. 5.

[29] Brawner, p. 339.

[30] *In the Valley of the Rio Grande*, p. 6. Efforts to locate this book at Dayton, Ohio, and Drew University in Madison, New Jersey, failed. Dr. John H. Ness of the World Methodist Historical Society and former E.U.B. Historian was also unable to help locate this valuable book of a bygone era.

[31] Letter from Lena Blake to Virginia Frank, Unpublished Papers, McCurdy Mission School. School officials estimate that at least ten children and five grandchildren of Mr. Gutierrez have since graduated from McCurdy High School.

[32] "Three New Workers for New Mexico," *Woman's Evangel* (January 1917), p. 7.

[33] Lillian Kendig Cole, p. 3.

[34] Richard C. Campbell, *Los Conquistadores: The Story of Santa Cruz Church*, Rev. ed. (Santa Cruz, New Mexico, 1968), p. 15.

[35] "Starting Work at Alcalde, New Mexico," *Woman's Evangel* (July/August 1917), p. 231. No author listed but obviously written by Miss Perkins.

[36] "Starting Work at Alcalde, New Mexico," p. 231.

[37] "Starting Work at Alcalde, New Mexico," p. 231.

[38] "Starting Work at Alcalde, New Mexico," p. 231.

[39] Dr. C. Whitney, "A Partial Glimpse of Our Home Mission Work," *Woman's Evangel* (June 1917), p. 181.

[40] Dr. P.M. Camp, "Santa Cruz Dedication," *Woman's Evangel* (November 1917), p. 341.

[41] Lillian Kendig Cole, p. 4.

[42] Campbell, p. 19.

[43] Paul C. Bailey, *A Biographical Sketch of Mellie Perkins*, United Theological Seminary, Dayton, Ohio. Unpublished Thesis and quoted in *Los Conquistadores*, p. 19.

[44] Mellie Perkins, *Woman's Evangel* (September 1913), p. 313.

THE MISSION REACHES OUT

August 1918 brought Miss Kendig rapidly back to Santa Cruz to assume responsibility as both principal and acting pastor. Traveling from Dayton to New Mexico with Miss Kendig was her new helper, Miss Ruth Smith. School opened at Santa Cruz on September 9 with fifteen pupils. Miss Kendig taught the upper grades and supervised the kitchen. Miss Smith taught the primary grades and was in charge of the dozen girl boarding students. At this time the boys and girls were divided, with the fifteen girls at Santa Cruz and the thirteen boys located ten miles north at Velarde under the supervision of Miss Bertha Wolheiter.

Life was rather hectic that year for many changes were taking place as the work of the mission caught on in the area. One of the most pleasant experiences was that of the first mission wedding between Miss Lottie Newman, a mission helper, and Mr. Charles Peterson, a very staunch supporter of the work.[1]   The wedding took place on July 18, 1918, in the new chapel by Rev. Callie King. Records indicate that the first funeral service held was that of Mr. John Womelsduff on October 19, 1918, and was conducted by Miss Kendig. Apparently his daughter was one of these early students for according to Miss Kendig,

> Early in the year one of our girls came to school late and said, "Miss Kendig, my father died last night. Will you come and conduct his funeral?" I immediately went to the Womelsduff home and made arrangements. A Methodist minister from Española assisted and we laid him to rest 'neath the blue New Mexico skies.[2]

The work was growing, and a full time pastor was needed for the three stations so the Home Board in Dayton sent the Rev. W.E. Dye and his wife. They arrived in time for the opening of school in the fall of 1919.

Great changes were occurring, and preachers obviously did more than preach.

> Rev. Dye had much to do as the maintenance manager. His wife was the boys' matron and many changes were made. The new Elco electric system was installed. Away with kerosene and gas lamps. What rejoicing when the electricity was turned on and the whole institution was electrified. What had God wrought. We were just his servants. But this wasn't all of our needs. The next year the Overmillers came and he installed water plumbing. Now, good-bye water buckets, outside toilets and all those

inconveniences and sanitation was possible.[3]

Life was obviously very difficult in those days, and medical help was not always available. The Petersons' new baby became ill the next year (1919) and died shortly after being baptized by Miss Kendig. She reports:

> There were no undertakers in the area. Mr. Peterson bought a casket at the general store and we prepared the body the best we could. We had a pastor then, Rev. W.E. Dye; and he conducted the funeral, and little Carl was buried in the mission lot. Later the church bought ground for a cemetery in Alcalde and he was moved there.[4]

Of a much more joyous occasion was the first infant baptism of a Spanish-American baby in the fall of 1919. One of the highlights of the year was the Confession of Faith at the altar on Easter Sunday, April 20, 1919, of the four Bustos girls (Ida, Onorata, Aurelia and Belen).[5]

In October a flu epidemic broke out. At first, according to Miss Kendig, outside students were banned but school went on for the boarding students. Shortly thereafter it hit even the boarding students. Velarde closed down sending the boys home. Miss Brawner and Miss Wolheiter moved to Santa Cruz to help with the ill. School was closed from October until December that year. Eventually everyone recovered from the flu and school resumed. Miss Carrie Short, a substitute for Miss Brawner, was the last to recover and taught the spring of 1919. Miss Dora Housekeeper taught at Santa Cruz for three months that same year.

The flu epidemic had one positive effect: it dramatically pointed out the shortcoming of keeping the boys at Velarde. Medical help was always at least twenty miles away. Velarde was just too far away from supplies and the building really was not equipped to handle a dozen or more young men.

> So the new plan was suggested to the board. They agreed and plans and blueprints were made. A contractor (a Mr. Anderson of Colorado Springs) was hired to build a large girls dormitory which would house forty girls and teachers and the first building built would hold thirty boys and the pastor and his wife. This definitely was the greatest step forward. Can you imagine what it took to furnish the new buildings and renovate the old. Then the students had to be enrolled. That was my job as principal.[6]

The financial picture and attendance figures give proof to the growing mission work of these days. Finances had increased from $218.24 in 1915, to $559.65 in 1916, and by 1919 totaled $3,664.46. Of this budget $3,000 was for misisonary appropriations, $330.50 was the pastor's salary, $60.00 for benevolence, $34.50 for local Sunday School expenses and $13.09 for local expenses. Sunday School attendance had risen from 11 in 1915 to 24 in 1916 and in 1918 stood at 59. Church membership was at 14 and church attendance was 44, up from 10 in 1915. Total enrollment for the entire eight grades at the three schools was about 75. Tuition was fifty dollars a year (boarding students) and many students worked at twenty cents an hour during school and part of the summer to pay their own way. Stories are still told of loads of potatoes and other produce that were used by parents to help partially pay for tuition.[7]

In many ways life was getting better at the mission school, and surely progress was being made in many ways, but opposition from the Roman Catholic priests of the area continued. In truth during these years the attitude of most priests in New Mexico was again that of hostility to the public school system and to any system that was not controlled by their church. From the Congregational Educational Society comes this insight of the times. A teacher writes,

> Our people are more persecuted by the priests for sending their children to our schools than they are in the villages where the priests do not visit so often. They never miss an opportunity to persecute the children as well as the parents, abusing them in public, calling them Protestants, and refusing to confess them and saying all manner of things against us.[8]

Miss Kendig expressed the opposition this way:

> Monday we opened school with fourteen enrolled. Here is the hardest battle. They tell us the priest preaches against the mission school every Sunday. Some of the folks are thoroughly scared. At noon a man came to tell us he had decided to send his three bright promising girls to our school. I almost felt like shouting. We are praying that another father will give his consent for his children to come also.
> ·
> Today two boys came and took their books, and with tears running down their cheeks said their mother was afraid the priest would be mad at her if she let them come here.[9]

Life was not easy for a young student at McCurdy in the early days.

Mr. Jose Manuel Martinez, one of the boarding boys at McCurdy in 1919 related that they often had problems with the Catholic boys at Santa Cruz Plaza:

> We had fights all the time…Mondays, after wash day (school was held on Saturday but not on Monday), in the afternoon we were allowed to go to town but we had to go in groups because the Plaza boys were always looking for us - they didn't want the Protestants there. I got beat up several times.[10]

It was difficult for students having stones thrown at them and being beat up, but this was relatively mild compared to the fate of those early Hispanics who converted to the Protestant faith.

> The life of a Catholic cast out of his church is a life of humiliation. He is thereby made an outcast not from the church only, but from society. His friends look down on him as an inferior… Altogether his life is made miserable for him.[11]

The letters which the teachers occasionally received from students made the effort all worthwhile. One such letter was reprinted in the November 1917 issue of the *Women's Evangel*. It was addressed to the Edith McCurdy Mission, Santa Cruz, New Mexico, and dated August 10, 1917. Excerpts are as follows:

> It would have been very impossible for me to learn anything if it hadn't been for the mission. My mother died when I was eight years old, so I have no one to teach me but the mission teachers…
>
> When I went to the mission school, I couldn't talk but a little bit of English…I learn to read my Bible and pray to God every day…
>
> I learn to love each other and many more things in the Home [Mission School]. When I finish my education, I will give God back the very best I have to give, and even now I am ready to do what he wants me to do. I am so glad to know all this things.
>
> I surely love my teachers and I know they are good to me…
>
> I want to be a teacher after I have finished my education. We live very far from the people. Oh, how I wish that we could have a church here![12]

Manuelita Martinez was fifteen at the time she wrote this letter. She had been one of the first boarding students and soon graduated from the eighth grade.

The fall term of 1920 was a happy one with the opening of the new girls' dormitory (Blake Hall today). It was a two story building with a large dormitory, five private rooms and a hospital room on the second floor. On the first floor was a large dining room, two reception rooms and a study room for girls. The basement consisted of a large and well lighted classroom, a furnace and coal room, a storage room, laundry and bathroom. All in all this was quite an improvement for the mission. Miss Kendig and Miss Smith were the teachers while Mrs. Dye and Miss Wilhide served as matrons.

In spite of a new building certain special problems faced the school. For example, Mr. P.M. Camp, Secretary of Home Missions, wrote to the readers of the *Women's Evangel* in November 1920 stating that "...of the fifty students enrolled in Miss Smith's room fifteen cannot speak a word of English."[13] A great deal of preparation work was needed with these students in spite of their eagerness to learn. For some students, almost everything was a new experience including sleeping in their first modern beds.

The religious part of the mission work certainly was not slighted. Records indicate that the chapel was full almost every Sunday. On Easter Sunday 1920, twenty members were received, and on Pentecost eleven more entered the fold. On Easter Sunday in 1921, thirteen new members were received. Additionally, there were three baptisms by sprinkling and twelve were baptized by immersion.[14] Miss Kendig wrote, "I'll always remember times when students accepted the call to come to the altar and become Christians."[15]

Miss Kendig and others were reaching out with the gospel to other areas. One of the earliest outreach trips was conducted by Miss Kendig and Miss Smith. They loaded up a portable organ in the buggy and drove north to Llano to the home of the Bustos family. Here they conducted services with Bible reading and singing.

Services with singing always brought out the children for they loved to sing gospel songs and to read the Bible.

In the summer of 1921 a rather strange event occurred at General Conference. Miss Kendig, who was attending as a delegate, was informed that the Santa Cruz church was not properly organized. This is somewhat bewildering for, as Rev. Richard Campbell has pointed out,

> *The Church Record* mentions that on February 6, 1921, when Rev.
> Dye was still pastor, the church was organized by the class

electing Miss Kendig class leader, Charles Peterson church
treasurer and Mrs. Charles Peterson church secretary.[16]
Today we can only guess at what it might have been that was not correct. In any event, Miss Kendig was allowed to remain at the Conference and proper documents were obviously put together in the near future.

The Rev. John Overmiller was serving a pastorate at Longmont, Colorado, in the spring of 1921 when he was called to serve in the mission field in New Mexico. Little did he know then of all the trials, tribulations and triumphs that the next seven years would bring. Rev. Overmiller has written that his first thought of doing work in New Mexico was during the years he spent at Bonebrake Seminary in 1918-1919. It was here that he became acquainted with Dr. P.M. Camp, then Secretary of Home Missions. However, one cannot help but wonder if the seeds for his work in New Mexico had not been planted sooner. It appears that Rev. Overmiller was attending Campbell College at the same time as Mellie Perkins (1909-1913). It is also a fact that Overmiller's elocution (public speaking) teacher was Edith McCurdy. Rev. Overmiller said in later years that he really benefited from Miss McCurdy's teaching and always remembered her statement, "When speaking to a group of people, always talk to those on the back seats and the rest of the crowd will hear you."[17]

Getting to New Mexico apparently was half the experience in those early days. Many are the tales of long train rides, lost baggage and unusual experiences by the early teachers, and the Overmillers were no exception. After holding an auction of all their household furnishings, except the essentials, which were shipped to Española by freight, the Overmiller family left Colorado.

> I had made provisions for camping out along the way. We made one bed from a canvas stretched across the backs of the seats, and another which would rest one end on the running board outside and be covered by a make shift tent. I had a small cupboard-like container attached to one running board. Some gallon tin cans, with holes in the sides, and sand in the bottom passed for a cook stove with gasoline soaked in the sand for fuel.[1]

Roads in 1921 were sometimes difficult:

> The trip over the Cimmaron Pass to Taos was a slow one because of a heavy rain which about drowned out the roads. We spent a cold overnight stop in a clearing along the way. I still remember

> how we shivered around our small camp fire while we cooked
> and ate breakfast.[19]

The Overmillers arrived, after a stop in Velarde, at Santa Cruz on July 6, 1921, ready to take up their new positions. Rev. Overmiller was to serve as the chief school Administrator as well as Conference Superintendent while Mrs. Overmiller assumed the role of boys' matron at Santa Cruz.

The mission property as of the fall of 1921 consisted of the following:

> ...a nice little church seating about one hundred people...

> ...a large building which was two stories above, a half under-ground structure which served as the girls' dormitory, dining room, office, living rooms etc...

> ...nearby was another rather large adobe building known as the boys' home. On the main floor was a living study room, a living room for the superintendent and family, with a kitchen off from it which was used as a bathing room for the boys instead of for cooking![20]

Keeping the students clean was no easy chore as indicated by the following statement:

> A boiler full of water was heated on the wood burning stove, and two wash tubs served to bath the children. A pump on the porch furnished the water - it was operated by hand.[21]

In addition to the downstairs living room the Superintendent's family had bedrooms on the second floor next to the dormitory which housed the boys. One could assume that this helped keep the boys quiet at night. There was also a double garage and a small building for a cow on the three acre compound. At Alcalde, ten miles to the north, the property consisted of five acres and a building which housed two classes and two mission workers, Miss Clippinger and Miss Wohlheiter. At Velarde, further north in the valley, there was a small chapel with two classrooms where Miss Brawner and Miss Blake held classes. At Santa Cruz classes were taught by Miss Kendig, who also served as principal, and Miss Smith. In sum, the mission picture consisted of three schools, six teachers, four matrons, a pastor and about two hundred students.

Staff members in 1921 could expect a salary of $500, and students were charged about twenty-five cents per month. The properties were valued at $50,000 and operated on an annual budget of $12,000. Most of the financial support came from the Women's Missionary Society.

Many were the needs of the mission school, for the schools were running at full capacity and showed signs of expanding. Money was scarce but Rev. Overmiller was creative.

> We had one cow, not a very profitable operation...We had a little money of our own, which we could spare, so I bought them [two cows], and charged the home for the feed and milk until they paid for themselves, then they became home property.[22]

Fall term saw the opening of the girls' dormitory, previously described, which was dedicated in November 1921 with Bishop Kephart and Rev. Overmiller heading the ceremonies. More room was needed for the boys, so additions were soon made for more sleeping rooms. One of the great luxuries for the boys was the new five stall shower room. Rev. Overmiller recalls how each newly arrived boy who went in for his first shower was greeted with cold water turned on full blast.

Student life with boys and girls together at Santa Cruz was always full of surprises. One former student of those days relishes telling what has become known in school lore as "the chicken coop story." It seems that three very active boys hid out in the chicken coop waiting for "lights out" before sneaking off to town. Rev. Overmiller found out where they were and quietly locked them in the coop. The boys had no choice but to break out later that night. The next day the guilty boys had to face a superintendent asking questions about who had broken into the chicken coop.[23]

Other student stories include tales of laundry days at McCurdy. Monday was the designated laundry day with school being held on Saturday to make up for Monday's absence. No one seems to know the origin of this schedule though it does seem to have to do with the amount of available hot water. That is, everyone could not be spic and span for Sunday and have the laundry done too. In any case Monday was wash day. The boys hauled the water to the girls' dorm, lower level. Then the girls did the laundry for themselves and a "little sister." After the washing the girls did their ironing and mending while the boys cleaned the buildings and grounds. Tuesday everyone went back to classes except the older boys who did their laundry. The boys did receive help from the matrons with the ironing of their shirts.

Cooking for the students was one giant job and certainly presented a real challenge to the women who reigned over the kitchen. With most of the students coming from a Hispanic background while most of the cooks, matrons and teachers were Anglo, one can imagine a real difference of opinion on food. Most students preferred dishes of beans and chile to almost anything else. Teachers lectured on nutrition and the cooks surely tried a variety of foods, but the regional taste buds usually won out. Girls were assigned certain mornings to help with the baking of bread. This meant getting up at four in the morning as forty loaves were needed each day. Additional baking was also necessary so that no work was done on Sunday.[24]

During the early years fire was always a threat at the school, and there was no fire department in the Valley. All the larger buildings were heated from coal burning furnaces and all the walls had wooden and adobe construction. Loading the furnaces was the job of the older boys, who frequently overloaded the coal. The result was overheated furnaces which could have burned down any building at any time. One more than one occasion Rev. Overmiller was called upon to man the fire extinguishers which were kept in every building. One day a fire occurred in the furnace room of the girls' dorm and what could have been a great disaster was quickly extinguished by the Superintendent. On another day the furnace in the chapel overheated. As the pastor relates it, "The furnace was so overheated that the walls around it were starting to burn and the wood around the registers at the end of the hot air pipes was burning."[25] This time it took longer to bring things under control, for the white hot furnace had to be cooled down. However, once again the pastor turned fireman saved the day. Some say that if they ever build a statue of Rev. Overmiller at the school it will be with a fire extinguisher in one hand.[26]

Student athletics were first organized at McCurdy during the 1920s. Rev. Overmiller is credited with starting the first baseball team in 1925. The first game was reportedly with Española. Basketball was officially organized later that same year by a teacher named Glen McCracken. Basketball in those days was played on outdoor dirt courts. Competitive games were played with nearby Santa Cruz and Española public schools and later expanded to include St. Michael's and the United States Indian School, both in Santa Fe. Girls basketball was organized, and they played against Allison-James and Loretto Academy, also in Santa Fe. Football first made its appearance in 1926 and was coached by Mr. Evans a local businessman. Games were played on the school grounds near the front of the campus (not the present football field). The first officially scheduled football game was lost to Menaul School of Albuquerque.

The heart of the mission school was its academic program. Both Rev. Overmiller and Miss Kendig sought constantly to improve the school's standards. By 1921 it was realized that while one eighth grade student was to graduate that year a large seventh grade class followed. So it was decided to begin a high school by adding one grade each year. Obviously much planning was needed to make this a reality. The curriculum was chosen with care so as to be accredited by the state. In the summer of 1922 Miss Kendig went to the University of New Mexico to study high school management, home economics and Spanish in preparation for the expansion. The tuition was raised at this time to $60 per year for grade school and $75 for high school students.[27]

At the commencement exercises in 1922, Manuel Martinez won the first prize of $2.50 in gold in the Oratorical Contest held by the Edith McCurdy Literary Society. The following students graduated that year: Nea Espinosa, Frank C. Garcia, Wayne Henderson, Victoria Martinez and Floripa Lujan.[28]

Rev. Overmiller was a very busy man during his tenure at McCurdy, for in addition to his school work he was the pastor at four different churches. He alternated preaching every other Sunday at Santa Cruz with Miss Kendig. Alcalde and Velarde had services in the afternoon and Española had services Sunday evenings. Indeed he had helped organize the church in nearby Española. It is interesting to note that at this time the United Brethren Church had taken over the work of the Methodist Church in Española.[29] Mrs. Overmiller gave music lessons and her students frequently played during school programs. Additional responsibilities for both of the Overmillers came in the birth of their third child, Vonda Mae, born October 1923 and officially the first "mission baby."

Former teachers and students alike remember 1923 as the year that the tradition of a Christmas breakfast for students first began. Apparently this tradition continued until recent years when size made it too difficult to handle. Late summer of 1923 also saw the school being used as the site of a Mission Workers Conference of the Southwest District including workers from all denominations.

The outreach of the mission school was extending farther and farther into the mountains and valley. On occasions Rev. Overmiller traveled to outlying villages such as Ojo Caliente and Abiquiu for services. As the pastor tells it,

> I had bought a saxophone and learned to play some church music with it. I had one "Anglo" boy who was quite good with a cornet. We made no announcement of our coming - there were no phones or newspapers in any of those villages at that time. We pulled up to the corner of the village square - set up our musical instruments and began to play...at the sound of our music heads popped out of windows, doors opened, and soon we had a crowd of some fifty people as we sang our message of religious songs. Then I gave a short message from the scriptures, using an interpreter, for most of the listeners knew no English.[30]

On another occasion Rev. Overmiller traveled into one of the remote villages. Finding that the only church was locked and had never had a service in it, because no priest would come that far, Rev. Overmiller proceeded to hold a short service outside the front door. A number of the students at McCurdy shared in these gospel outreaches of Rev. Overmiller. Serving frequently as assistants and interpreters were Jose Martinez, Candido Medina and Victoria Cruz.[31]

This was not to say that the mission outreach was going unopposed - quite the contrary as the whole community was always under the surveillance of the Catholic Church. Rev. Overmiller states, "They would go to great lengths to discredit anything the Protestant Church was doing."[32] One example had to do with a Santa Cruz couple with a child in the mission school. It seems that the local priests were very angry at the parents for sending the child to the school. When the father died unexpectedly, the priest refused burial in the only cemetery unless the child was pulled from the mission school. The mother refused and the father was buried outside the wall. According to Rev. Overmiller,

> When the mother continued to rebel, he [the priest] had unsacked lime placed underground at the grave site. He told the mother that her husband was burning in purgatory. To prove it, he took her to the grave, made a hole with a rod down into the grave, then poured water into it. Of course, it boiled out.[33]

Crude methods such as these worked in the area for awhile primarily due

51

to the legacy of superstition.

Transportation was a problem for the school from the beginning. The first year at Santa Cruz everyone walked. The second year Miss Perkins bought a car, but this left with her in the summer of 1918. The school (Miss Kendig and Miss Smith) purchased a horse and buggy. When Rev. Dye arrived with a car the horse named "Nell" was sent to Velarde. Rev. Overmiller had an old Ford which he insisted that Miss Kendig learn to drive. Later Rev. Overmiller purchased a new Overland and Miss Kendig, with the aid of the other teachers, bought a Model T Ford. This car was promptly nicknamed "Henry" and was the source of both many trips and stories. As Miss Kendig reports, "He was overturned, stuck in water, stranded in sand, and stuck out on the prairies, but it was all helping to do the will of the Lord."[34]

The hauling of supplies from Española to Alcalde and Velarde moved from a horse and wagon in the early years to a small trailer pulled by Rev. Overmiller's car. The coal supplies were hauled in by teams and wagons hired from the Petersons, Mardorfs and Jake Johnsons. On one occasion Mr. Mardorf's horse died, and the school reimbursed him $50 for the loss. All of these families were kind friends to the mission. Mr. Johnson ran the nearby dairy from which the school purchased the milk needed in addition to their own production.

Rev. Overmiller as Superintendent of the New Mexico Conference was required to visit each church and hold a quarterly conference. To service the churches out on the plains meant traveling over the Sangre de Cristo Mountains with dirt roads all the way. This was a round trip of about 200 miles and took at least two days in travel time. Some of these trips were more than just routine experiences.

> One night a terrible rain storm came up and we had to dole people out to stay with others who lived closest to the church. The pastor and I were left to sleep in the church. I chose a church bench. The pastor slept on the floor with a rug pulled over him for warmth. He was a big, heavy fellow and was quite a sight.[35]

Rev. Overmiller was once caught in a real blizzard and along with the local pastor went to spend the night with a church family. It seems that their room was on the cold north side, facing the wind and snow. "The pastor slept in his clothes, but I could hardly afford to wear wrinkled clothes for the rest of my trip, so I undressed and shivered throughout the night."[36]

Once on a survey trip of the Protestant work being done by the United Brethren, Rev. Overmiller had a car full of Methodist and Presbyterian officials when they got stuck in the middle of one especially deep stream. Apparently the high water had shorted out the current to the spark plugs. What was one to do? Never at a loss for effort, Rev. Overmiller reports that he did not want to have all those city folks get wet, so he climbed out on the running board over the fender to the top of the radiator, reached down and turned the crank. "Sure enough, with the help of their prayers, which I am sure they were saying, the motor started and we were on our way."[37]

As the mission school grew the need for more room became obvious. Records indicate that the first property at Santa Cruz purchased by Mellie Perkins was done so with the help of Mr. John Block. Intermediaries of local merchants and friends were necessary for any land purchases for years due to the opposition of the priests. In 1925-26 a four acre plot of land, which makes up the front of the present campus, was purchased with the aid of a Mr. Murphy.

Numerous improvements occurred during the Overmiller tenure. Among these were the construction of a new home and office for the superintendent, the dedication of the new girls' dormitory, an addition to the boys' dormitory, erection of a power plant for electric lights, remodeling of the chapel at Velarde, construction of a two-room school at Velarde (1927) and establishment of a new church in Española. Perhaps the greatest improvement brought about by Rev. Overmiller was that of an improved water and sewage system. As the superintendent tells it,

> Everything in those early days was very primitive. Our water supply at the boarding school in Santa Cruz, except for drinking water, came from ditches, and was stored in cisterns. We drilled another well and installed two pumps which gave us good service.[38]

Some might say that the most noticeable addition to the mission, at least sound wise, in these years was the addition of a church bell. Rev. Campbell relates in his history of the Santa Cruz Church that, "The congregation wanted so badly a 'Protestant' church bell, so money was pledged by the congregation and solicited in the community."[39] The bell arrived in the valley by train and was not very successful as the bell could not be heard.[40] As usual Rev. Overmiller was resourceful and with the carpentry help of Mr. Johnson they raised the bell tower up so that all could heard the bell ring. And ring it did - for years.

The year 1926 is special in the history of the school, for it marks the first graduation class of high school seniors. The six members of that class included Guillerma (Willie) Chavez, Elzadie Leese, Adelina Martinez, Jose Manuel Martinez, Candido Medina and Robert Vialpando

Rev. Overmiller wrote the following about this first class:

> When September of the same year came around I took four of them in my car to York College in York, Nebraska, from which some of our workers had come and where I knew some of the teachers. I made arrangements for them to enter college, found accommodations for them, and means by which they could earn part of their tuition.[41]

According to J.M. Martinez, a member of this first class, five of the six members attended York College and the sixth (Robert Vialpando) attended Indiana Central. Adelina Martinez and Elzadie Leese stayed at York one year while three of them (Chavez, J.M. Martinez and Medina) graduated four years later.[42] Each of these three former students served at one time or another at McCurdy as teacher, coach and principal. Robert Vialpando became an ordained minister and later taught for the Santa Fe schools.

Alcalde was the newest mission station in the valley, and during the 1920s work seemed to move slowly. According to Rev. Overmiller this was not due to the lack of dedicated teachers, for surely Miss Lula Clippinger (1920-31), Miss Freda Rasor (1924-26), Miss Wolheiter (1918-24) and Miss Florence Warren (1926-30) were as untiring as any who served. But rather it was the general lack of education among the people. As has been reported this mission consisted of about five acres of land, a two-room school house and living quarters for two workers.

Due to the lack of a proper burial ground in the valley for Protestants, a cemetery was started at Alcalde. Old customs died slowly, one of which was the act of rushing to the new grave upon lowering of the casket and throwing or kicking chunks of dirt down upon the grave. On one early occasion Rev. Overmiller remained in the grave until his helpers had quietly shoveled a fair amount of dirt into the opposite end. However, "...just as soon as I was out of the grave three or four children rushed up and kicked dirt into the grave - it was their custom."[43]

Velarde, at the northern end of the valley, had continued the mission work since its inception by Miss Perkins. The boys had been moved to Santa Cruz some years before but Miss Mary Brawner (1915-25), Miss Anna Hardy (1918-22) and then Miss Lena Blake (1922-31), carried forth the good work.

Like others before her, Miss Blake had felt the call of the Lord to the mission field during her youth in West Virginia. Through an article in *The Telescope* she volunteered her talent to Rev. Overmiller and hurried West. Due to a mistaken ticket master she entered the valley via Denver and Walsenberg, Colorado, and the narrow gauge railroad.

Miss Blake got off at Velarde where she was met by Miss Brawner and a horse and buggy. She was welcome company for opposition from the local priest was discouraging to say the least. One of her students said it well when he smiled at her and said, "We like to hear you teach the Bible, but it is pretty hard on our parents who have to be scolded by the priest every time they go to church."[44]

One of the great stories from Velarde was told years later by Miss Blake. It seems that a boy in Miss Brawner's room announced one morning that his father was coming to school to make the teachers stop teaching the Bible. After thoughtful prayer by the teachers he was graciously received when he arrived. They sang some hymns which he seemed to enjoy and then Miss Brawner said, "I shall read the lesson about Abraham from the Catholic Bible. The students will use the English King James version and I shall give you a Spanish Bible."[45] It appears that they had a good lesson and when the time came to write he quietly bowed himself out the door. Once again the Lord and kind words had saved the day.

Frequently the teachers at Velarde were called to render emergency service. With a horse named "Nube" and a wagon they would transport patients either north to the Presbyterian Hospital at Embudo, a trip of six miles, or south the sixteen miles to Santa Cruz. The only phone in the community was located in the mission home.

A touching story is related by Miss Blake concerning the illness of a young grade school girl named Susana Garcia who became ill on the last day of school. She continued to waste away all summer and eventually the doctors gave up on her. During morning devotions the Misses Brawner and Blake decided it was time to turn to the Lord for healing.

> We invited Susana's uncle, Mr. J.R. Luna, who was our Sunday School Superintendent and treasurer, to go with us. He did, and prayed in Spanish for her. We prayed in English and anointed Susana in the name of the Father, Son, and Holy Ghost.[46]

Several weeks later after attending church conference in the eastern part of the state, the teachers returned and found Susana entirely well.

In 1925 Miss Brawner retired to Danville, Illinois, after serving ten hard years. Miss Cora Newman served at Velarde as teacher from 1922 to 1935 and Miss Delia Herrick taught from 1923 to 1929. Miss Sarah Brooks and Miss Myrtle White each taught for a year at Velarde. In1927, thanks to help from the Christian Endeavor of the East Ohio Conference, a school was constructed. The following year the Hauser Chapel was remodeled and dedicated just in time for the first meeting of the Advisory Council.

This new body, the Advisory Council, met semiannually to review the United Brethren New Mexico Mission work. Membership included a representative from the Mission Office, the Conference Superintendent (Rev. Nichols), Professor Glen F. McCracken. Rev. Overmiller, and principals of each school: Miss Lula Clippinger (Alcalde), Miss Delia Herrick (Velarde) and Miss Vera Herrick (Santa Cruz).[47]

In the spring of 1927 a series of moves was begun that eventually brought about a number of changes at the mission. In order to assist the Overmillers a new pastor, Rev. Harold Megill, was appointed to the Santa Cruz circuit. The family's furniture was shipped and stored at Española, but for the summer months the Megills were assigned to Amistad. Mrs. Megill (Pearl Testermann) was no stranger to the Santa Cruz mission for as a volunteer she had worked at the school during the flu epidemic in the winter of 1920-21. Their work at Amistad was obviously successful. By the time of Annual Conference in August laymen from Amistad requested the Bishop to let the Megills "stay put" which they did, but they also added the Sedan church to their duties. By ordinary process the Megills would have been transferred to Santa Cruz; as it was, Rev. and Mrs. C.C. Gish took over the charge. Mrs. Gish took over preaching at Española while

Mr. Gish served Santa Cruz, Alcalde and Velarde. They served the area until 1929. Local sources believe that this arrangement was not too satisfactory and the Española church actually disbanded for awhile.[48]

The Overmillers requested another assignment from the field which had demanded so much for seven years. "The job was telling on our strength so we decided to let up a bit... The Home Mission Board asked me to take on the job of opening up a new church in Albuquerque."[49] So it was that at the close of the 1927-28 school year the Overmillers left the valley to which they had given so much. Less than a year later Rev. Overmiller resigned his position as Conference Superintendent to accept the presidency of York College of York, Nebraska, a position he served with distinction for another decade.

NOTES

[1] Lillian Kendig Cole, p. 5.

[2] Lillian Kendig Cole, p. 5.

[3] Lillian Kendig Cole, p. 8.

[4] Lillian Kendig Cole, p. 6.

[5] Campbell, p. 19.

[6] Lillian Kendig Cole, p. 7.

[7] Campbell, pp. 19, 43; and Frank, p. 16.

[8] Leaflet of Congregational Education Society quoted in *Women's Evangel* (October 1916), p. 338.

[9] Lillian Kendig, "Opportunities in New Mexico, as Seen by a New Worker," *Women's Evangel* (November 1916), p. 383.

[10] Interview with Jose Manuel Martinez, Antonito, CO., May 11, 1981.

[11] "Domination of the Priesthood in New Mexico," *Women's Evangel* (Octdober 1916), p. 338.

[12] Manuelita Martinez, "Thankful for the Mission School," *Women's Evangel* (November 1917), p. 342. Manuelita's father, Albino Martinez, was converted as a young man at an evangelistic meeting in Colorado and was threatened more than once for his strong evangelical beliefs.

[13] P.M. Camp, "The Opening of School at Santa Cruz, New Mexico," *The Evangel* (November 1920), p. 325.

[14] Campbell, p. 20.

[15] Lillian Kendig Cole, p. 9.

[16] Campbell, p. 43.

[17] Letter from Rev. J.R. Overmiller to Miss Virginia Frank, 1965.

[18] Overmiller Papers, part of an unpublished manuscript entitled, "From Here to There," McCurdy School files, believed to be written in 1977, p. 11.

[19] Overmiller Papers, p. 11.

[20] Overmiller Papers, p. 11.

[21] Overmiller Papers, p. 11.

[22] Overmiller Papers, p. 12.

[23] Interview with Jose Manuel Martinez.

[24] Frank, p. 27.

[25] Letter from J.R. Overmiller to Miss Virginia Frank, undated, p. 3.

[26] Frank, p. 27.

[27] Lillian Kendig Cole, p. 8.

28 *The Evangel* (July-August 1922), p. 215.

29 *The Evangel* (September 1923), pp. 232-233. The Methodist Church had ceased operation several years before and transferred their property to the United Brethren for the $800 mortgage.

30 Overmiller Papers, p. 14.

31 Campbell, p. 21.

32 Overmiller Papers, p. 12.

33 Overmiller Papers, p. 12.

34 Lillian Kendig Cole, p. 4.

35 Overmiller Papers, p. 14.

37 Overmiller Papers, p. 14.

37 Overmiller Papers, p. 15.

38 Overmiller Papers, p. 13.

39 Campbell, p. 22.

40 Campbell, p. 22.

41 Overmiller Papers, p. 13.

42 Interview with Jose Manuel Martinez.

43 Overmiller letter to Frank, p. 3.

44 Blake Papers, p. 4.

45 Blake Papers, p. 5.

46 Blake Papers, p. 5.

47 "New Workers in New Mexico," *The Evangel* (November 1928), p. 300.

48 Campbell, p. 23.

49 Overmiller Papers, p. 16-17.

THE McCRACKEN ERA

The departure of the high school principal, Mr. Joseph G. Howe, and his wife who served as the school matron, after only one year of service (1925-26) created a new vacancy on the staff. As fate would have it, the young man who filled this position was destined to mold and shape the mission school for nearly the next forty years. His name was Glen F. McCracken.

McCracken, a native Texan, had been teaching in the Española public school for three years prior to the vacancy at the mission. He was well-known to the school for both his coaching ability and his interest in a certain young teacher by the name of Miss Violet Munns who had come to the school in 1922.

Within the year both the McCurdy and Española schools offered this promising young educator the position of principal within their systems. In a discussion with Rev. Overmiller, serious doubts were raised by McCracken as to whether the mission job was for him since "He hadn't been a church goer before converted in the Española United Brethren Church."[1] Rev. Overmiller must have been convincing, for McCracken soon accepted the position with the McCurdy School. One factor in McCracken's decision to come to McCurdy soon became evident, for the pretty Miss Munns became Mrs. McCracken in September 1926.

Following their marriage both McCrackens left New Mexico for the entire 1926-27 school year. They attended Indiana Central College where Mr. McCracken obtained his A.B. degree. The McCrackens were back at McCurdy for the opening of school in 1927 when McCracken assumed the responsibility of high school principal.

Within a year there were other changes at the school. Rev. Overmiller moved first to a new church in Albuquerque and then on to the presidency of York College in Nebraska, and McCracken was appointed to the position of superintendent. At the same time, Rev. Maurice Nichols of Colorado was appointed to the superintendency of both the New Mexico and Colorado United Brethren Conferences. The records indicate that the mission workers in the schools for the year 1928 were as follows: Superintendent - Professor McCracken; Santa Cruz High School - Miss Vera Herrick, Mrs. W.A. Allen, Mr. Lowell P. Herrick; Grade School -Miss Whrelda Wrye, Miss Gertrude E. Hamaker, Mr. W.A. Allen; Matrons - Mrs. Nancy Smith, Miss Zella Herrick and Mrs. Jess Clark;

Alcalde - Miss Lula Clippinger and Miss Forence Warren; and Velarde Miss Delia Herrick, Miss Cora Newman and Miss Lena Blake.

In an article to the faithful readers of *The Evangel,* McCracken fondly reviewed his first year as superintendent. He wrote of the difficulties of opening days, of memorizing new names and of language problems. But he also reported good attendance and a good atmosphere. Students were being turned away due to the lack of room, especially boys - but still they came.

> One old man came and wanted to put his grandson in school. He said the lad had been in a public school for five years and hadn't learned a thing - "Nada Palabra! Nada Palabra!" he repeated many times. The boy was too bright looking to turn away, so room was made for him.[2]

The church membership at Santa Cruz was also growing as the pastor reported twenty-eight new converts. The Senior Christian Endeavor class had a membership of fifty-nine and the Junior Endeavor had a registration of thirty-nine. It seems that a number of young people were carrying the work of the mission into remote regions of Northern New Mexico.

A 1928 news story recounts the experiences of one of the first school graduates as follows:

> She is in the hills about forty miles west of us. We are very proud of her. She has thirty-seven pupils and only nine single seats; the rest must sit on a few benches. None of these pupils are above the fifth grade for none can speak English and teaching from English textbooks is a slow process. She has no equipment. We gave her some storybooks and games we had left from Christmas. She has no church privileges and nothing that is elevating or helpful. Drunkenness runs riot and sometimes she is afraid to venture outside her door...[3]

By 1930 the Great Depression was upon the entire country. Life certainly was not easy on the mission field, and yet that summer a new outreach was started at Vallecitos. For some time several students from that little mountain community, whose name in English means "Little Valleys," had been urging the establishment of a grade school. Prominent among those doing the urging were Candido Medina, a member of the first high school graduating class and later a high school principal at McCurdy, and Albert Amador. The Amador family, which throughout the years has helped the mission school, even offered a home in which classes could be held and in which a teacher could be housed.

So it was that Miss Delia Herrick and Miss Gertrude Hamaker were transported by Superintendent McCracken up into the mountains at Vallecitos to the house provided by the Amadors and another mission was started. During the week the house was a school and on Sunday it became the church. Miss Herrick was the cook and social worker that first year, while Miss Hamaker taught school and preached in Spanish.

In 1931 Miss Lula Clippinger came to Vallecitos after eleven years of service as a social worker at Velarde. Miss Lula, as she was known, was born in Franklin County, Pennsylvania, and had been a missionary to Africa prior to coming to New Mexico. She became a real "workhorse" for the mission, building fires for both school and church, cooking for the mission, preparing the kerosene lamps and, after a hard day of work, calling on future members. For sixteen years Miss Clippinger set a pace that was hard for fellow workers to match. Many homes in the most remote regions surrounding Vallecitos received a visit from Miss Lula on horseback.

That same year a church congregation of forty-four members was organized and, after a few years of hard dedicated work, it was deemed necessary to build a church. Ground breaking ceremonies occurred during July 1936.[4] Mr. Olsen, a Christian builder from Denver, and Dr. Maurice Nichols undertook the church construction with a great deal of free labor coming from the members. Heavy rains more than once threatened to ruin the adobe construction, but by April 11, 1936, enough of the church was completed for a dedication service. About three hundred people attended this special service, including Bishop Statton who became the first Protestant bishop ever to visit Vallecitos. The building was named the Wiggin Memorial United Brethren Church in honor of Miss Wiggin who gave the first $200.

This structure was unusual in several ways. It had the first stained glass windows ever seen in the community. These were provided by one of Miss Lula's Pennsylvania congregations. The building also had fine pews in an age when many New Mexican churches had none. Additionally, it had a beautiful oil painting done by Mr. Aruthur Williams of the Avondale Church in Columbus, Ohio. The painting was of Christ the Good Shepherd (El Buen Pastor); and Miss Lula believed that the artist had been divinely guided, for the trees resembled local trees, the sheep were appropriate, and the canyon in the background looked familiar.[5] This painting remains a cherished part of the Vallecitos heritage today. Many parts of this remote church were furnished by donations of various Pennsylvania churches including the pastor's study which came from the women of the Hershey charge.

For many years the Vallecitos church continued to grow in spite of the fact that it had no ordained minister on a regular basis. Various services, including funerals, were cared for by the mission workers, with a pastor traveling up from Española when possible. During the fall of 1938 a primary school was opened for twenty-five lively young students under the teaching of Miss Jane Norris. While workmen were repairing the school, the one-hundred-year-old original walls of the service room were torn down amid local tales of buried gold.[6] No gold has ever been found in the walls or on the mission ground, but there has been real gold in the love and dedication of the teachers, preachers and service workers who have labored at Vallecitos.

From the early days of Mellie Perkins, the Velarde Mission continued to serve the community. McCracken reported that in the fall of 1930 the school had an enrollment of forty-seven students under Miss Blake, Miss Brooks and Miss Newman.[7] Life was never easy at Velarde and during the Great Depression years of the 1930s it was even worse. Mr. and Mrs. Candido Medina, who served at both Velarde and Alcalde from 1931 to 1935, reported that one bright spot was the "community play nights" which they used as a method of bringing people into the mission.[8]

Rev. I.E. Caldwell, a former missionary to Puerto Rico who served as pastor to Velarde and Alcalde from 1937 to 1940, reported that the staff then consisted of Miss Elnora Freshly at Velarde and Miss Eleanor Scheaffer and Miss Marie Langdon at Alcalde. Rev. Caldwell's daughter Evalina, a recent graduate of York College who taught at Velarde for part of a year, reported to the readers of *The Evangel* what was to become a trend in the education field of the area. She wrote, "Quite a number of Christian teachers trained in mission schools are to be found among the public school teachers and their influence will be felt."[9] Indeed this has been the case, and for a number of years in the 1930s and 1940s the majority of the area's public school teachers were McCurdy Mission School graduates.

By 1943 there were nearly eighty students enrolled at Velarde, which

Miss Edith McCurdy, about 1910.

Right: Santa Cruz, 1915. First Mission Building.

*Far right: Blake Hall, 1917
Classrooms, dormitory and kitchen*

Bottom: Student Group, early 1920s.

*First row: Edna Martinez, Emilia Lujan,
Adelina Martinez, Florepa Lujan, Celia Herrera.
Second row: Alfredo Garcia, Chiz Martinez,
Lowell Howell, Solomon Martinez.*

Bottom right: Manual Arts Class, early 1920s.

*Left to right: Richard Alire, Alfredo Lopez,
Robert Vialpando, Apolinario Valdez, C.E. Medina,
Chic Martinez, Juan Lovato, Onofre Sanchez,
Clifford Wolf, Melcome Sargent*

*Top: Conference of workers at
Velarde Mission, 1921-22.
Left to right: Vera Herrick,
Mary Brawner, Mrs. Dye,
Rev. Dye, Lena Blake.*

*Top right: Rev. Overmiller and
the basketball team, 1926-28.*

*Right: Class of 1926.
First row: Elzadie (Leese) Rhodes,
Robert Vialpando, Guillerma
(Willie) Chavez.
Second row: J.M. Martinez,
Adelina (Martinez) Griego,
Candido Medina.*

Bottom right: School picnic, 1927.

Miss Gertrude Hamaker's class, 1929-30.

Mission staff, 1930.
First row: Mr. Shilling, Mrs. Shilling, Nicolassa Martinez, Effie Kneafe,
Mary (Neal) McIntyre, Zella Herrick, Guillerma Chavez.
Second row: Harold Jeffers, Lena Blake, Wilma Brandstetter, Glen McCracken.

Senior class of 1941.

Teachers' room, 1947.
Left to right: Dorothy Miller, Emily Keck, Helen Ball, Helen Butterwick,
Irene Cole, Cecil Walker, Charlene Sanders

School Staff and family, 1948-49.

McCurdy Mission barn, 1940-1950s.

Poland China pigs, the 1940s.

*McCracken:
First Place winner
for pigs, 1950s.*

Top left:
Second and third grade class,
1954-55 (class of 1964-65).

Bottom left:
McCracken Gym, 1953

Top right: Girls' dorm,
hair-fixing time, 1962.

Bottom right: Elementary
Principal, A.W. Pringle and
student Shelly Sawyer, 1974.

Alcalde Mission

Velarde Mission

David Burgett and Dale Robinson, 1982-83.

Vallecitos Mission

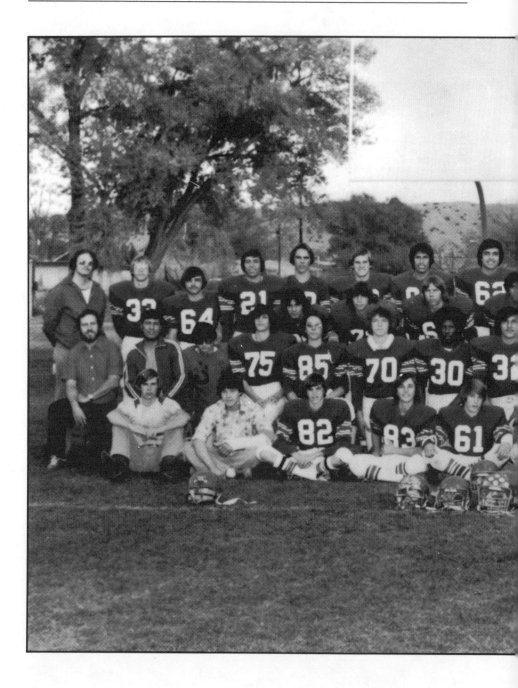

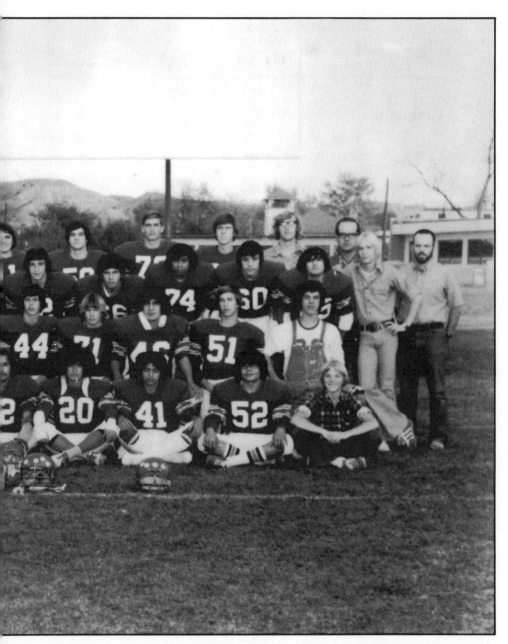

State Champion Football Team, 1976.

State Champion Girls' Volleyball Team, 1982-83.
Left to right: Lenna Monge, Martha Cordova, Daven Quelle, Renee Finch,
Sally Shockey (coach), Julie Burgett, Yvonne Ellington, Liz Naranjo.

was really more than could be adequately handled though many of the parents were unable to understand why the school could not admit everyone. Miss Georgene McDonald, who served as principal for a number of years, was forced to refuse late admission to Spanish-Americans and Anglos alike, and she did so with both grace and equality.

In 1937 McCracken referred to Alcalde as "...one of the fields where our mission work is appreciated most."[10] The workers were appreciated for many reasons: giving first aid, transporting people to the doctors, serving as midwives - the list is endless. Miss Pearl Wolford, who served as both teacher and principal from 1939 to 1945, described the mission station as "...like stepping into a different world. Surrounded by mountains on all sides."[11] She told her readers about the regular morning devotions, the hymns sung, the Bible stories and prayer time. It appears that each teacher had four grades and they averaged about seventy-five pupils each year. According to Miss Wolford, each day brought its joys and sorrows, its successes and its failures. She wrote, "Each day we pray for strength to teach the pupils in our care as God would have us do."[12] Christmas time was the happiest time of the year at the school, for each student received a Christmas package made possible by the many mission boxes sent by various Otterbein Guild Chapters.

After many years during which the school, church and living quarters were all housed within one building, additional space was created in 1943. A teachers' cottage was provided by the West Virginia Conference in loving memory of Miss Maria Langdon who, at the time of her unfortunate death on August 14, 1939, was serving as the principal at Alcalde. She was only thirty-three at the time of her death, but she had already served eight years on the mission field. Miss Delia Herrick says of her, "She was a faithful Christian, good teacher and nurse, and the people will miss her.[13] Glen McCracken called her "A hard worker who gave her best to this work and the people of New Mexico."[14] Her replacement wrote, "As long as Alcalde remains, Miss Langdon's memory will be held sacred by the people here."[15]

The construction at Alcalde in 1943 allowed for more classroom space; however, by 1950 the total enrollment had dropped to a low of twenty-nine. This was due in part to the court ruling of what is commonly known as "The Dixon Case." The case challenged the right of Roman

Catholic nuns to teach in the public schools of New Mexico. In handing down its ruling the District Court barred one hundred thirty-nine nuns from teaching in the public schools. The case was appealed to the State Supreme Court but was dropped when Archbishop Byrne withdrew all nuns from the public schools at the request of the State Board of Education. Interestingly enough, during the following year the enrollment at the mission school started to climb again when parents and students realized that the ruling had not markedly improved the public education system.

The opposition to the Alcalde Mission from the local Roman Catholic priests was as strong in the 1930s and 1940s as it had been in the earlier years. Frequently children dropped out of the school at the time of their first communion; otherwise, the priest would not perform the service. Sometimes brothers and sisters also dropped out for the year.

Ironically, one of the duties workers at Alcalde were frequently prevailed upon to perform was burials. Miss Avis Williams recalls that soon after she arrived at Alcalde in 1945 a knock came on the door and a little girl said, "Our baby died. Do you have any boards or any paper or pretty cloth?"[16] She goes on to say, "We had the funeral the same day as the fingernails and lips were turning purple. There weren't any morticians around. The closest funeral home was in Santa Fe so they were buried in the little box."[17]

There was no embalming of any kind being used in New Mexico in those days; and if services were held in the school house, as they frequently were, it was quite hot. Teachers who served Alcalde said that on more than one occasion as the minister preached the funeral service they could see his nose start to curl up due to the odor of the deceased. Miss Williams reports, "If the child died and the family hadn't had the baby baptized and they were Catholic, they would crawl under the fence and bury them in the Catholic cemetery. Sometimes they would ask the mission teachers to come to the house and have a little service before they did this."[18]

Throughout the years of the Great Depression the mission school at Santa Cruz continued to grow. McCracken reported a fall enrollment in 1930 of one hundred eight. Thirty-nine of these students were in the high school, making it larger than ever before.[19] However, the number of boarding students dropped to sixty-five, which probably reflected the local economy. All in all these attendance figures are remarkable when one considers that some sixty per cent of the Spanish-speaking villagers were on relief during these depression years.[20]

Community relations were always important to McCracken, and many local stories are told of his particular handling of a difficult situation. One of the favorite stories concerns a rock-throwing incident at a graduation service. It seems that a local young man heaved a large rock through the chapel window, narrowly missing Mr. Amador. The men at the service charged out of the church and prepared to give the young man a thrashing. McCracken would not stand for this sort of action. Instead he took the culprit to the district attorney in Santa Fe who found him guilty and fined him. McCracken then lectured the shaken young man and invited him to become a friend of the school. Numerous incidents of this nature occurred and, through careful handling, improved relations with the community did begin to develop.[21]

The year 1931 turned out to be one of the most dramatic in the history of the school due to the great gymnasium fire. For many preceding years students and faculty had labored long hours in order to raise the necessary funds for constructing a much-needed gym. Then, with tragic timing, just as final completion was occurring, the building burned to the ground. So dramatic was this loss to the mission that for years afterward events were dated from the time of the fire - November 12, 1931.[22] According to local folklore the one positive result was that the fire served to bring about the creation of the Española Fire Department.

The ruins were still smoking when McCracken made the decision to rebuild. Records indicate that the school collected $7,500 in insurance money and started reconstruction immediately. When interviewed years later, McCracken indicated that lumber was $20 a thousand, brick was bought at a low price from the State Penitentiary in Santa Fe and the sand and gravel came from the nearby Santa Cruz River. McCracken and Dr. Maurice Nichols, the District Superintendent, supervised the rebuilding.[23] Depression-day finances did make it necessary to place temporary roofing on the reconstructed building. Years later, when replaced, the old shingles became *objets d'art* and were sold by the school in various forms. Reconstruction was successful; and when Bishop A.R. Clippinger came for graduation services in the new gym, he told readers of *The Evangel* that "This commodious building would do credit to many college campuses."[24]

In May of 1940 this gymnasium was dedicated and officially named "McCracken Gymnasium," an honor well deserved.

At the time of its completion this was the only gymnasium from Santa Fe to Taos. Always conscious of public support and community goodwill, McCracken invited the Española public school and the Santa Cruz Catholic school to share the gym for athletic events. Area residents were both surprised and pleased by this generous ecumenical gesture and soon annual basketball tournaments became one of the area highlights. Today it is generally believed that this gymnasium was responsible for breaking down much of that which had separated the mission and the community. However, a building can only do so much good, so truly we must say that the real deciding factor in the new era of goodwill was the personality of Glen McCracken. This remarkable man also found time from his many duties to become an ordained United Brethren minister in 1938, and the following year completed his Master's Degree in Education at the University of New Mexico. Some years later he was awarded an honorary doctorate from York College in Nebraska.

Throughout the decade of the 1930s regular United Brethren pastors served the four mission churches. Rev. and Mrs. Walter Lobb served from 1929 to 1931, and Rev. and Mrs. Wilbur York worked in the area from 1931 to 1933. It is rather remarkable that in 1931 the Rev. Clarence A. Schlotterbeck returned to pastor the same valley into which he had ridden on horseback in 1910 while searching for Protestant homesteaders. During his ministry the Alcalde and Velarde churches were separated from the Santa Cruz circuit. It is sad to note that this rather lonely bachelor was tragically killed in an auto accident in Colorado while returning from the Annual Conference.[25] Surely somewhere in the Española Valley today there is room for a historical marker to the memory of this concerned pastor.

The Rev. and Mrs. George Richter, former missionaries to Africa, served at Santa Cruz from 1938 to 1941. During their ministry regular church services were started in the mountains at Tres Piedras and Petaca. The Rev. Richter is best remembered for the many worthy things that he did for needy people as well as for mingling with the townsmen to get them to come to church.[26]

It was during these years that Mrs. McCracken and others started the Spanish Prayer Group, with services in both the McCurdy Chapel and in private homes. These Spanish-language services have continued through the years and have become a regular feature of the Santa Cruz United Methodist Church. Indeed the blending of two languages in the worship services has served to emphasize man's oneness under God.[27]

On the eve of World War II McCracken reported that student applications to all of the schools were plentiful with Santa Cruz having record enrollments in 1938 and 1939. Alcalde too had many students and actually had to cut back some. Both Velarde and Vallecitos also had large enrollments. This apparent success came not as the result of some advertising campaign but because the people had confidence in the schools. Indeed not only were they full accredited by the State Department of Education but also they were receiving many commendations for the quality of their programs. It was with pride that Superintendent McCracken wrote to the readers of *The Evangel* in 1939, declaring that:

> The students of our schools are rapidly taking over the places of leadership in the communities where they live. The people want them to do this, realizing that their characters, ideals, and aspirations are above average. A few days ago we passed through the county seat and stopped at the court house. Six of those holding offices and assistant offices were graduates of Mission schools. Approximately one hundred sixty students have graduated from the high school here. Many of these are in places of responsibility in teaching, government and other walks of life.[28]

Frequently visitors arriving on the McCurdy campus for the first time were surprised to find green lawns, uncommon for much of New Mexico, and a thriving orchard filled with apples, pears and peaches. Thanks to the long irrigation ditch which brought the precious water all the way from the Sangre de Cristo (Blood of Christ) Mountains miles away, the orchards and vegetable gardens prospered at the school. Compared to much of the nearby landscape, the mission grounds looked like the Garden of Eden.

The agricultural program was a special and unique phase of the school having been started by Rev. Overmiller during the 1920s. The cows were used to supply the milk and butter, and pigs were added to help with the garbage disposal. When Mr. Arthur Pack of Ghost Ranch fame enrolled his son at the school, he also gave a financial gift of $3,000 which was used to buy registered Jersey cows and swine. Some years later the farm switched to Holstein cows for a better yield of milk. The most important aspect of the animal program was that the offspring of the registered livestock were sold to the students and others, thus helping to improve the livestock in the entire valley.

Throughout the summer months much time and energy went into food preparation for the boarding school. Zella Herrick, long-time mission teacher and principal (1923-64), wrote that during the summer of 1942 they canned over 500 quarts of cherries as well as 1,000 quarts of peaches, apricots, plums and pears. Fifty gallons of apple butter and jam as well as large quantities of jelly, pickles, tomatoes and vegetables were prepared. Additionally some 109 pounds of butter were processed. Considering the fact that a normal summer also included the cleaning, varnishing and painting of the buildings, one can see that there was not much wasted time.[29]

Improvement to the farm program were always taking place and in 1939 the old dairy barn was torn down. A new and larger barn was constructed further north on the campus, and silos were added. By the mid 1950s pasteurized milk from the school cows not only supplied the staff and students but the hospital as well. Special milk-bottle caps read, "McCurdy Grade A Pasteurized." Down through the years many McCurdy students have had their own personal memories regarding the milking and caring of the farm animals.

No mention of the McCurdy farm program would be complete without a few words regarding McCracken and his hogs. They were not just hogs but Registered Poland China hogs, and prize winners at that. The one-time Texas rancher delighted in the school hogs and was never happier than at State Fair time. In 1950 he went to Albuquerque for the Fair with ten hogs and came home with eight first-place ribbons, three seconds, two thirds, two fourths and two grand champions. This total of seventeen premiums for ten hogs had to be some kind of state record.

In many ways the boarding school was the "heart" of the mission, for it was around these students that so many of the activities were centered. Principal Zella Herrick told her readers in 1943, "...if we had two more dormitories the size of these we have we would still have to say 'no more room' before we wanted to."[30] Each year throughout the 1940s it seems that there was more pressure to enlarge the boarding school. An average year found about forty-five girls and thirty-five boys living at the school. Normally most of the boarding students were teenagers, although there is the record of Ercilia Cordova who became a boarding student at the age of three because her sisters were at the school. The young girl's father paid one of the older students in the dorm to iron her clothes, take care of her hair and help when needed.

After a normal day, evenings found all the students in chapel services. Teachers and students led in songs, prayers and short inspirational talks. The youngest students went to bed after chapel services, while the older ones usually had an hour-long study period. Teachers frequently reported that students would sing choruses after retiring to their darkened dormitories. Saturday evenings were special play nights with all manner of activities ranging from quiet games to more active ones in the gym. The local community students as well as the boarders participated in most of these activities.

Of the many loyal teachers and matrons who served in the dormitories surely Miss Lena Blake is in a special class by herself. Originally from West Virginia, she taught at Velarde for nine years until her health weakened. She then asked McCracken to try her for one year as girls' matron. She ended up staying on that job for twenty-five years. Miss Blake started with nineteen girls under her care in 1931; and the numbers increased each year until they reached fifty-four in 1956, the year she retired. Words cannot adequately express the love and Christian concern that Lena Blake gave to the mission through her thirty-four years of service (1922-1956).

It also took a very special person to handle the thirty or more boys living in the old Herrick House. Such a person was Miss Irene Bachman who, along with her mother, helped to make the dormitory into a real home for the boys. Stories are still told by McCurdy graduates about Miss Bachman making them clean the dorm at night due to some misbehavior after the lights went out.

The boys ranged in age from ten to twenty and in any given year at least half of them were old enough to shave. With one bathroom and only two small mirrors in the dorm, it was a difficult situation. The dormitory had become crowded and uncomfortable; and as the numbers edged upward, six boys were assigned to each room. Through the pages of *The Evangel* in 1943, Miss Bachman shared her needs and concerns for a new dorm with the church body. Her dream dormitory, for the most part, came true in February 1950 with the construction of a new building. Since

1965 this dormitory has been named Bachman Hall in honor of Irene Bachman and her twenty-two years of service to the school (1929-1951).

Throughout the years the cost of maintaining the mission increased steadily. For example, in 1942 the yearly budget for the five schools was $9,000, plus the salaries for eighteen workers totaling $12,000. One year later the operational costs went to $16,000 and salaries to $18,000. Tuition likewise had to be increased almost annually. Beginning at $50 per year for boarding students in 1915, it was increased to $88 in 1942, to $95 in 1953, to $175 in 1955, and then to $540 in 1967. Elementary day-school students could expect to pay $6 per year in 1942 while the high school day-student paid $12. In 1943 these figures were raised to $7 and $13; in 1955 they increased to $10 and $15; and by 1966 they increased again to $90 and $140. Even with these almost annual increases, the amount paid by student tuition in no way covered either the true cost of the education nor the dormitory expenses. The Home Board estimated that their total annual investment was 17¢ a day per pupil in 1942.[31]

Student tuition was paid in cows, sheep, potatoes, hay, melons - whatever a family had available. Students have always worked at the school both during the school year and in the summers to help pay for their tuition. During the depression years the school was forced to use a large amount of mutton prepared in many different ways. It seems that the students did not object too much to helping with the butchering until the sheep fat was used in the cooking.

During the early years the mission workers who came to New Mexico accepted their positions at $50 a month and paid $5 a month in rent. By the depression years of the 1930s, salaries had not increased significantly; and during the worst of times the workers frequently went for months without pay. Some months only $5 and $7 came in for their food allowance. During the spring of 1933, Miss McDonald and Miss Langdon at Alcalde ran out of both food and money. The morning in which they had eaten the last of the food, a little girl came to their door with a bucket of fresh peas and told them, "Mama said for you to come and get vegetables from our garden when you want to." They said that they learned anew the meaning of "The Lord will provide."[32]

At the height of the depression McCracken was faced with a $200 debt and no money with which to pay it. It is reported that he prayed over this matter for some time. A short time later a check for exactly $200 arrived from Mr. Richard Houser, Sr. It seems he had gotten some insurance money back and thought that McCracken and the school could use it.[33]

Salaries had improved by 1943 when the Home Mission Board Secretary U.P. Hovermale could report that single teachers, nurses and matrons would receive $600 to $720 per year. Married teachers would receive $1,000 to $1,200, as would pastors and missionary evangelists. The same report urged churches to support one of these workers or to provide a scholarship for some boy or girl who might not otherwise be able to attend.[34] School buildings were valued at $60,000 at Santa Cruz, $10,000 plus at Vallecitos, $9,000 at Velarde and $5,000 at Alcalde.

With the coming of World War II, a number of events were set into motion that were to change forever the slow-moving, out-of-the-way region of Northern New Mexico. History records that the first two National Guard units activited and sent to the Philippines were the 200th and 515th Coast Artillery battalions (strange for a land-locked state) of New Mexico. Thus when the Japanese conquered the Philippines, more than a quarter of the men killed or captured were from New Mexico.[35]

Meanwhile, up on the Pajarito Plateau, almost within sight of the McCurdy Mission, a new city was beginning. When J. Robert Oppenheimer was asked to help select an isolated spot for the country's first atomic laboratory, he remembered an early back-packing trip to the Jemez Mountains and his visit to the Los Alamos Ranch School.[36] By 1942 the Los Alamos Scientific Laboratories were established and at work developing the atomic bombs which were to help end the war. The opportunities for local residents to help build and maintain this massive operation have economically changed the entire region.

New money began to flow into the Valley and the ripple effect was soon seen in the construction of new homes, shops and roads. Some local people maintain that the creation of Los Alamos changed the region more than any other single event in local history. Before Los Alamos, local wages for manual labor were about $1.00 per day; but with the construction at Los Alamos wages increased drastically. One McCurdy student made more money during his two-week Christmas vacation, even with paying union dues, than mission teachers made in two months.[37]

Son of an early pioneer minister's family. Rev. Albert L. Brandstetter

and his wife served the Española and Santa Cruz churches during the war
years 1941-46. Soldiers from Los Alamos came down into the valley
from "The Hill" on Sundays, and some found their way into the local
churches. One Sunday morning on his way to Santa Cruz from Española,
Rev. Brandstetter picked up a young soldier who said that he was looking for the United Brethren mission. "I introduced him in the service that
morning and all the people took him in and invited him to dinner. He
came down with others quite regular to the church service."[38]

It appears that this hitchhiking soldier would come in the morning to
teach a Sunday School class and stay all day. The soldier was Lawrence
Taylor, who went on to become a pastor in Detroit and later a Conference
Superintendent in Michigan.[39]

The realities of the war came home to the mission in many ways. Lula
Clippinger reported from remote Vallecitos:

> We have some interesting children with keen ears. The other day
> five girlies came to the house. They were much excited. They
> likely had learned by papers and radio of the trial "Black Out" in
> Santa Fe. It took a good many words to quiet them that no bomb
> would drop here.[40]

By 1942 there was a teacher shortage, and McCracken took over
much of the athletic coaching. It is interesting to note that the local draft
boards considered sports to be good training for future fighters and thus
allowed the school buses enough gasoline to be used for athletic transportation. The school curriculum was adjusted to meet the requirements for
pre-army and pre-war training. Many students who were later drafted or
volunteered wrote back to the school stating that their schooling at Mc-
Curdy had given them good opportunities for advanced training in the
military.[41]

For many at the mission the arrival in 1941 of Miss Anna A. Schafer
as the first school nurse was an answer to prayer. Hailing from
Washington, D.C., and having served in Africa and Arizona, Miss Schafer
was well qualified to observe the local health conditions. In her first report
she wrote:

> The infant mortality rate in the State of New Mexico is higher
> than that of any other state in the Union. Malnutrition is
> prevalent among the children. This past week, through the
> W.P.A., hot lunches were served to the children at the noon hour.

Soon we will see a gain in weight when they get this extra food. In many of the communities there is no doctor available...

Everywhere there is evidence of a lack of sanitation in the houses. Flies are taken for granted as a necessary evil. Screening is rarely seen on doors or windows. This may account for a great many of the infant deaths from dysentery.[42]

At the time of Miss Schafer's arrival no room was available for a clinic within the mission; so for $5 a month, two rooms without water or bathroom facilities were rented in an old, run-down house near the school for a temporary clinic. health classes were started in all grades and Red Cross first aid was soon taught to interested students and adults.

Construction of a new clinic building on campus took place in 1942. This was a special project of the Women's Missionary Association. Additionally the June 1942 Love Offering of the Otterbein Guild helped to equip the clinic.[43] Mr. and Mrs. Arthur Pack of Ghost Ranch donated six beds and mattresses and Mrs. J.R. Engle and friends gave $1,000 for improvements. Miss Lillian Moffat, a nurse from Monessen, Pennsylvania, was added to the staff in 1943. In writing to the readers of *The Evangel*, she described the operation procedures of their tonsil clinic, stating that the doctor usually started to operate at 5:00 A.M. and was usually finished by 8:00 A.M. Patients were kept for two days to watch for bleeding. She pointed out the dire need for a health room at each school.[44] No funds were available for expansion of the health work to the other schools, and before 1943 was over Miss Schafer was called into active duty with the Army.

During the war years the Packs of Ghost Ranch began urging local people to consider building a hospital in Española. The challenge to the United Brethren Church was that the Packs would provide the necessary funds on the condition that the church would staff and operate it as a mission hospital. Mr. Frank Willard of the Bond and Nohl Company of Española deeded the church a twelve-acre tract of land for the hospital site.

Surely the Lord was at work on this project, for through the urging of Arthur Pack and Dr. S.G. Zeigler, then General Secretary of the Board of Foreign Missions, young doctor Samuel Zeigler and his wife stopped in New Mexico following his discharge from the army. While serving in the South Pacific and in occupied Japan, Dr. Zeigler had been urged by his father to consider the Pack offer in New Mexico. As the good doctor tells it, "I was taken with the countryside and challenge and I told Pack that I would give two years to start a hospital."[45]

So it was that in September of 1946, with Dr. and Mrs. Zeigler and Miss Moffat, the small clinic at McCurdy became in fact a hospital. The clinic-hospital was swamped with sick babies with the first new birth coming early in October. Mrs. Zeigler served as bookkeeper, secretary and nurse. Both Zeiglers served as ambulance drivers to the hospital in Santa Fe. For over a year the Zeiglers and their two sons lived in the clinic before moving across the street to the new Santa Cruz parsonage.[46]

Meanwhile the hospital, with a sizable grant from the Packs, was under construction. Church officials, who at first balked at the Pack offer of tobacco company stock for funds, soon changed their opinion as the Packs joined the Española church and Arthur helped with the formation of the hospital.[47] When Dr. Sam (as he is known locally) arrived, he oversaw the planning for the building and designed a hospital with a core. Rev. Paul McFarland from the Dayton office served as the superintendent of construction with Mr. Peabody from Ghost Ranch overseeing the work. On May 8, 1948, the 32-bed hospital was dedicated with a host of church and state dignitaries on hand.

The hospital opened its doors with a professional staff of fifteen missionary doctors and nurses. Dr. Zeigler called them "...a wonderful collection of people from Ohio, Pennsylvania, Wisconsin and Michigan."[48] All were on the low missionary salary and a number have given most generously of time and talent to both the hospital and the mission school. For example, Dr. Leonard Akes, one of the original mission doctors, has done so much without pay for the mission staff. A number of hospital workers certainly deserve special recognition including Ruth Specht, who set up the nursing department and stayed ten years; Dorothy Vogel, who served twenty-eight years before retiring in 1980; Lois Coover, who has worked in the office since 1950; and Barbara Martin who has served as a nurse since 1951. Dr. Zeigler never left his adopted new home, having delivered over 4,000 babies in the Española area. Today the 100-bed hospital, which is independently managed, serves as a monument of love to the community.

By the end of World War II, Rev. and Mrs. William Young were serving the Santa Cruz circuit, which was finally broken into two separate congregations: Española and Santa Cruz. By the time that the vote was taken at Johnstown, Pennsylvania (November 1946), to merge the Evangelical and United Brethren Churches, the work at Santa Cruz had been in existence for thirty-one years with no separate house of worship for the community. Eighty-one church members met with the students in the McCurdy Chapel, the second-oldest building on campus, which by now was entirely too small and inadequate. At the Quarterly Conference that year Mr. C.E. Medina, chairman of the building committee, reported that $6,500 had been pledged and there was $1,600 in cash on hand toward a new church.

Dr. U.P. Hovermale (for whom the current elementary building is named) told the readers of *The Evangel* that $25,000 would be needed for the new building and equipment. The Otterbein Guild Love Offering of June 1946 went toward this project.[49] After years of praying and planning and eight months of construction under the leadership of local contractor Ralph Valdez, the new building became a reality. Former Santa Cruz pastor Richard Campbell tells that $15,000 worth of free labor was donated by the pastor and local congregation. Dorm students and local men helped to pour the cement. All of the painting, the staining of ceiling boards and the installation of pews was done by the congregation. Baccalaureate services for McCurdy were held in the new building in 1953, and on July 26 Bishop D.T. Gregory officially dedicated this lovely new sanctuary.[50] Within a few years stained glass windows were added to the church, thus beautifying it even more.

Since its construction the Santa Cruz church has served as the hub of much of the religious activity at the mission school. School chapel services are regularly held in the sanctuary. Youth Fellowship, Boy Scouts, Red Cross and Bible School have all been held within the church and parsonage. At least two local men have entered the ministry from the Santa Cruz Church. They are Rev. Harold Sanchez, who has served at Hernandez, and Rev. Lewis Brown, originally from Indiana, who served the Ojo Caliente circuit.

During the years of 1954-59 Rev. and Mrs. Andy Jordan served Santa Cruz. Participation, attendance and finances all seemed to improve; but minor troubles kept life interesting as discussed in the Winter Quarterly

Conference meeting of 1956:

> Motion by Rev. Brandstetter that we refer the matter of the horses
> getting on the church lawn to the Board of Trustees and suggest
> that every trustee call higher authorities regarding the matter.[51]

Under the leadership of Rev. and Mrs. Richard Templeton, 1959-61, the Santa Cruz charge continued to grow. An Every-Member Canvas was held in 1960, double Sunday morning services were launched and a building committee began to study plans for a new educational unit. These plans came to fruition under the leadership of Rev. Richard Campbell and the new $50,000 educational unit was dedicated on March 17, 1963.

Meanwhile up at Vallecitos, the year 1947 saw the end of an era with the retirement of Miss Lula Clippinger after twenty-seven years of dedicated service. Miss Clippinger had been not only the mainstay of the mission, which had the largest membership of any of the Spanish-speaking churches, but also had ridden horseback through the mountains to hold services at such places as Ancones and Cañon. Her reliable Spanish-language translator was usually Max Trujillo, whom Conference Superintendent Nichols called "a faithful servant of God."[52]

> Years came and went - and so did the mission staff. Some have
> come and stayed through the years. Some have come and served
> and gone. So it was that on Saturday, Sept. 20, 1947, the Pringles,
> a new family from the Ohio Sandusky Conference, arrived at
> Vallecitos. After car trouble, jacknifing their trailer in a sandy ar-
> royo, and too many bumps the tired little family got the key to
> their new home about 9:30 P.M.[53]

Their "new little home" had no electricity, no running water and no indoor plumbing. Heating and cooking were done with a big wood stove. The new pastor, Dolph Pringle, and his wife Gwen were both born in Ontario, Canada. They met and fell in love at church-related Otterbein College where he was class president (1940) and she was class secretary. Married in 1942, Dolph served a church in Sandusky while attending Oberlin Seminary. Gasoline rationing forced Dolph to ride the Greyhound bus to the church and to use a bicycle to visit his congregation.[54]

Like many newly married Eastern couples, they took a trip "out West." While visiting Albuquerque, they were persuaded to give a young missionary teacher a ride up to McCurdy and thus saw for the first time the area that, unknown to them at that time, was to be their future home.

Back in Sandusky their church was visited by Nellwyn Brookhart who had just come for a year's work at Vallecitos. She told of the needs there, and in a very short time the Pringles were on their way to New Mexico. Their 1937 Plymouth took them up the unpaved roads of northern Rio Arriba County to Vallecitos where they became the only Anglo family in town.

The Pringles recall that they ate a lot of pinto beans that first year; and since theirs was the only car in town, it served as the ambulance. A highlight for the Pringles occurred when Dolph's Johnstown, Pennsylvania church sent them money for a washing machine. He had the Maytag machine converted to a gasoline motor so they could utilize it. After two years, fifty-eight flat tires and two broken clutches, the Pringles transferred to the McCurdy main campus at Santa Cruz.[55]

Through the years the school at Vallecitos normally held classes for the primary grades only. However, in 1951-52, a fifth grade was added and then a new class each year until all eight grades were held. Enrollments reflected the expanded offerings, moving upward from twenty-eight in 1932-33 to forty students in 1953-54. However, the burning of the local sawmill in 1957 saw many families forced to leave the community to seek employment elsewhere and enrollment sagged. Once again only the lower grades were taught. Strange as it may seem the 1960s saw an influx of new people into Vallecitos. Many were "free spirits" or "hippies," but they had children; so once again all eight grades were offered at the mission school.

The late 1940s saw the McCurdy Mission reach out to a number of the more remote communities, primarily through the efforts of Rev. Roy Carpenter. Starting out as the boys' dormitory supervisor, Carpenter says that upon the death of Dr. I.E. Caldwell (1942) he prayed, "Lord, send me; and I, Carpenter, began to study Spanish."[56] Local sources credit him with being instrumental in the pioneer work at Chamita, El Rito, La Madera, Ojo Caliente and Petaca.[57] Rev. Carpenter would circuit ride the region on Sundays, always covering well over a hundred miles. He held preaching services in homes and urged the children to attend the mission schools. During the summer months Bible Schools were held at each station with help from McCurdy teachers such as Irene Cole, Helen Ball and Lillian Vermillion. Miss Cole recalls that at Petaca in 1945 they had to utilize an old building that had been partially burned out and which had no doors.[58]

During the 1950s a number of college students from Otterbein and Lebanon Valley participated in the Bible Schools under the Evangelical United Brethren Summer Service Project. At Hernandez an additional outreach was started by some of the missionary nurses from the new Española Hospital, and a few years later Rev. Harold Sanchez continued the work at both Hernandez and Chamita.

With the dedication of the Hovermale Memorial Elementary School on May 22, 1963, another milestone was reached at the McCurdy Mission. Dr. U.P. Hovermale, past Executive Secretary, Board of Home Missions and Church Extension of the Evangelical United Brethren Church, had witnessed a deep interest in the mission program in New Mexico. Construction of this fine facility was made possible by the 1962 World Service Day offering and other speical gifts.

The year 1964 and 1965 turned out to be big retirement years, as C.E. Medina, the high school principal, Miss Zella Herrick, a long-time worker, and Glen F. McCracken bid adieu to the school. Medina represents one of the many McCurdy success stories. Born in Vallecitos, Candido Medina entered the boarding school as a sixth grader and was one of the six members of the first graduating class in 1926. Medina went on to graduate from York College in Nebraska, where he met and married his wife, Ethel. Both worked at Alcalde and Velarde for four years. Medina worked in the local public school for many years and then served as McCurdy's high school principal from 1951-64. Both of the Medinas' sons are McCurdy graduates. The Medinas continued to be very active in the Santa Cruz Church after retirement. C.E. Medina died on April 22, 1978.[59]

Having answered the call to New Mexico from Rev. Overmiller in 1923, Miss Zella Herrick served as a teacher at Santa Cruz until 1929 when she was promoted to school principal. In 1946 she relinquished that position to work in the school office until her retirement.

Zella had been preceded to New Mexico by her sister Vera in 1922. Vera taught at Santa Cruz from 1922 to 1929 and again from 1933 to 1934. She went to Velarde for two years and returned to Santa Cruz for the 1942-43 school year. Another sister, Miss Delia Herrick, labored at Velarde from 1923 to 1929 and then continuously from 1930 to 1959 at Alcalde, Santa Cruz and Vallecitos. A younger brother, Lowell, came to the mission and taught at Santa Cruz from 1927 to 1929. The Herricks were all from the Kansas City University Church where their father was a minister. Totaled together, the Herrick family labored some eighty-nine years on the New Mexico mission field - a record par excellence and unsurpassed in school history.

There comes a time when every era must end, and so it was that in 1965 the McCrackens retired from the leadership of the McCurdy Schools. For almost forty years Glen McCracken's strong hand had expertly guided the work of the mission. Growth in the number of buildings, the size of the student body, the quality of instruction and the number of programs highlighted this era. As Superintendent of McCurdy, Sunday School teacher, community worker and a loyal soldier for our Lord, Glen McCracken epitomized the purpose of the mission school. Indeed on one occasion a man was overheard addressing Dr. McCracken as "Dr. McCurdy" -so closely had he allied his life with his work.

Throughout the years Dr. McCracken's wife Violet had been a loyal fellow worker and companion, frequently serving as a substitute teacher, always without pay. Mrs. McCracken had reared two children, Patricia and Phillip, and served as the gracious hostess to hundreds of visitors who came to the school. She also actively served many local civic and church organizations.

On June 5, 1965, the *New Mexican* (Santa Fe paper) carried the following statement in big, bold letters:

> Dr. Glen McCracken, Congratulations! Your former students congratulate you for the valuable service which you have rendered McCurdy School in particular and the Española Valley as a whole during the last 40 years. We have learned to think of you as a permanent part of McCurdy school and it will seem rather strange after you have retired. We know that your Christian attitude toward all people regardless of racial origin is something real and not a show and it is precisely for this wonderful quality that people of all our three cultural groups in this Valley love and respect you. We wish you a very happy retirement.[60]

The next day more than 500 people attended the retirement reception on the McCurdy campus. Representatives from the local Chamber of Commerce, Jaycees, Kiwanis, Rotary Club, Lions Club, Garden Club, Women's Club, United Church Women, 4-H, Alumni Association, P.T.A. and student body were in attendance. Among the many honors bestowed on Dr. McCracken was one of special recognition by Jack Campbell, Governor of New Mexico.

Glen McCracken remains a legend at McCurdy. He departed this life on July 26, 1976, but as the *McCurdy Message* so aptly phrased it, "So long as McCurdy's doors remain open to serve the young people who come to her, Glen McCracken will never truly leave this valley."[61]

NOTES

[1] Frank, p. 38.

[2] "A Year in One of Our Spanish-American Schools," *The Evangel* (November 1928), p. 314.

[3] "News From New Mexico," *The Evangel* (April 1928), p. 109.

[4] Lula Clippinger, "Intimate Story of Vallecitos, New Mexico," *The Evangel* (November 1937), p. 311.

[5] Clippinger, p. 311.

[6] Lula M. Clippinger, "Visiting Homes in Home Mission Territory," *The Evangel* (December 1930), p. 341.

[7] Glen F. McCracken, "Report of Beginning of New Year in New Mexico," *The Evangel* (December 1930), p. 341.

[8] Interview with Mrs. C.E. Medina, Española, New Mexico, May 6, 1981.

[9] Evalina Caldwell, "Day Schoolwork in the Upper Rio Grande," *The Evangel* (November 1937), p. 311.

[10] Glen F. McCracken, "Recent Advances in the Spanish American Mission Schools of New Mexico," *The Evangel* (November 1937), p. 308.

[11] Pearl Wolford, "My First Year at Alcalde," *The Evangel* (November 1940), p. 306.

[12] Wolford, p. 306.

[13] "Olga Marie Langdon," *The Evangel* (November 1939), p. 304.

[13] "Olga Marie Langdon," p. 304.

[15] Wolford, p. 307.

[16] Interview with Miss Avis Williams, Española, New Mexico, May 11, 1981.

[17] Interview, Williams.

[18] Interview, Williams.

[19] McCracken, "Report of Beginning," p. 341.

[20] *In the Valley of the Rio Grande*, p. 3.

[21] Frank, pp. 42-43.

[22] The correct date of November 12, 1931, has been verified by the school "weather notes" kept for many years by Mr. Mardorf and now by Mr. Hilton. The erroneous date of 1937 has been used in a number of sources. Special appreciation goes to Marge Wickersham for this clarification.

[24] Frank, p. 44.

[24] Bishop A.R. Clippinger, "Home Missions in New Mexico," *The Evangel* (November 1938), p. 296.

[25] Campbell, pp. 23-24.

[26] Campbell, p. 24.

[27] Campbell, p. 24.

[28] Glen McCracken, "Our Spanish-American Schools," *The Evangel* (March 1939), p. 302.

[29] Zella Herrick, "Again in the Whirl at Santa Cruz," *The Evangel* (November 1943), p. 299.

[30] Herrick, p. 300.

[31] *In the Valley of the Rio Grande*, p. 10.

[32] Interview with Miss Georgene McDonald, Española, New Mexico, May 12, 1981.

[33] Interview with Mrs. Violet McCracken, Santa Fe, New Mexico, May 1981.

[34] *In the Valley of the Rio Grande*, p. 28.

[35] Harold J. Alford, *The Proud Peoples: The Heritage and Culture of Spanish-Speaking Peoples in the United States* (New York: David McKay Co., Inc., 1972), p. 158.

[36] Roland A. Pettitt, *Los Alamos Before the Dawn* (Los Alamos, New Mexico: Pajarito Publications, 1972), p. 58.

[37] Interview with Rev. A.L. Brandstetter, Los Alamos, New Mexico, May 14, 1981.

[38] Interview, Brandstetter.

[39] Campbell, p. 24.

[40] Lula M. Clippinger, "The Crowning Part of a Vacation in Getting Back Home," *The Evangel* (November 1941), p. 310.

[41] Zella Herrick, "Opening Days in New Mexico Schools,' *The Evangel* (November 1942), p. 306.

[42] Anna A. Schafer, "New Mexico Health Program Starts," *The Evangel* (November 1941), p. 312.

[43] Dr. U.P. Hovermale, "Surveying the Home MIssions Field," *Religious Telescope* (March 21, 1942), p. 14.

[44] Lillian M. Moffat, "Are You Mindful of Them," *The Evangel* (November 1943), p. 301.

[45] Interview with Dr. Samuel Zeigler, Española, New Mexico, July 8, 1982.

[1] Interview, Zeigler.

[1] The Española Church was originally located on Railroad Street near the

present day hospital turn off. A service station stands there today and the congregation is the present day Valley View Church.

48 Interview, Zeigler.

49 Dr. U.P. Hovermale, "Our Need of a Sanctuary at Santa Cruz," *The Evangel* (May 1946), pp. 156, 158.

50 Campbell, pp. 25-26

51 Campbell, p. 26.

52 Rev. Maurice Nicholas, "Colorado-New Mexico Conference News," *Religious Telescope* (December 22, 1945), p. 23.

53 *Viva la Mision* script used for 50th anniversary historical pageant in 1962, p. 15.

54 Interview with Rev. and Mrs. A.W. Pringle, Española, New Mexico, May 15, 1981.

55 Interview, Pringle.

56 Rev. Roy P. Carpenter, "A Waiting Harvest Field," *Religious Telescope* (March 21, 1942), p. 13.

57 Interview with Rev. A.W. Pringle, Española, New Mexico, July 1, 1983.

58 Interview with Miss Irene Cole, Española, New Mexico, July 1, 1983.

59 Interview with Mrs. Ethel Medina, Española, New Mexico, May 6, 1981.

60 Joyce Rohde, "Dr. and Mrs. Glen McCracken Honored," *World Evangel* (August 1965),. p. 250.

61 *McCurdy Message,* The McCurdy Schools Bulletin, September 1976, p. 1.

THE MISSION EXPANDS AND FACES THE FUTURE

Several years prior to his actual retirement, McCracken had notified the church board of his pending decision. But who could take his place? Who could succeed an institution? After so many years of service, McCracken and McCurdy were almost synonymous. Slowly the church wheels began to turn and after much thoughtful prayer the final decision was made - Dale E. Robinson would be the fourth Superintendent of The McCurdy Schools.

Robinson was born in Joplin, Missouri, in 1929, the eldest of five brothers and a sister. His father was a construction worker; and since the Depression made work difficult to find, the family moved almost every year. Having to prove himself in each new school Robinson grew up fast and tough. High school graduation was from Springfield, Illinois, and college work was completed at church-related Indiana Central.[1]

During his college years football was certainly one of Robinson's fortes. He was named to both the All-State and National N.A.I.A. teams. As a physics major he had planned a teaching career, but the United States Army had other ideas. Drafted in 1952, Robinson ended up at White Sands Proving Grounds where he received his first introduction to New Mexico.[2]

During the 1953 Christmas holidays, Robinson married his high school sweetheart. The summer of 1954 found the soldier and his bride, Margaret, living in Alamogordo, New Mexico, and spending every opportunity sightseeing the Southwest. "We thought that we would never be back," recalls Margaret. The Lord surely works in mysterious ways, for one of their outings included a trip to Española and McCurdy. Margaret's father was an E.U.B. minister and her mother had once dreamed of teaching at McCurdy. During the Robinsons' brief visit at the school, they met Irene Cole and the Pringles. Little did any of them every dream that in the near future they would all be colleagues at the mission.[3]

Following his Army discharge, Robinson taught at Fancy Prairie, Illinois, in Springfield, and then in Decatur. During these years, he received a Master's Degree in counseling from Illinois State University. In 1959 the Robinsons were back at Indiana Central with Robinson working in the Admissions office. For two years he performed all sorts of admission tasks, and it was from this position that he accepted the offer at McCurdy.[4]

Prior to his actual move to Santa Cruz in August of 1965, Robinson received periodic correspondence from McCracken with the letters usually ending "decision awaits your arrival." The decisions awaiting arrival even included the colors of paint for the girls' locker room. In actuality a number of major decision had already been made in Dayton. The foremost change was the decision to end the entire farm program. Although it was a source of pride for both school and community, the mission had outgrown the original concept of self sufficiency through the farm products. Española had grown and private homes now surrounded the original mission grounds. It appears that hog pens and dairy barns did not make urban neighbors very happy and local pressure grew against having livestock within the city.

Devoid of emotional attachment the farm was no longer economically profitable. Unfortunately down through the years the farming aspect of the mission had never received state approval for its activities. During the late 1940s and the 1950s there were some discussion regarding the feasibility of becoming a vocational school, but nothing specific emerged. By the time of Robinson's arrival the farm animals had been sold and the barns were empty. By 1965 the majority of McCurdy graduates were bound for colleges and not for the farms.

In making the decision to move to McCurdy, Robinsons had worried about the education of their three children (Steve, Mike and Lisa - a fourth child, Kyla, was born at the mission). Years later, reflecting on this early concern, Robinson indicated that his children had received far more in the way of bilingualism and biculturalism than they had ever dreamed of receiving. All of the Robinson children turned out to be outstanding students and athletes.[5]

Among other things an interesting procedure awaited the new superintendent in the area of bookkeeping. It seems that two sets of books were kept, one for the farm and one for the school. The official detailed records were managed by Miss Herrick but in actuality McCracken was the walking financial record. Since the mission staff received their pay checks directly from the Dayton office, extensive records at McCurdy were unnecessary. In essence the checkbook stubs were the real indication of the school's financial status.

For a budget the mission locally made up its list of needs and submitted it to the Home Office. Once Dayton accepted the budget the church supported it. For example, in 1965, some 76% of the total budget was paid for directly by the church in monthly checks to the school. Faculty members were also paid by mail and on more than one occasion the checks arrived a week or so late due to the lack of church funds. Salaries were not high for anyone by any standard. Single faculty members could expect $2,600, while married teachers got $3,200 for a twelve-month year. All faculty did receive housing, utilities and a medical policy, but there was no retirement plan. Teachers going back east for the summer could expect an extra month's pay to help with expenses and were expected to speak to as many churches as possible. Staff members remaining on campus were obliged to help with the maintenance of the school. Other chores also included care of the apple and cherry orchards and canning. All of the food purchases had been a McCracken responsibility and what he bought the school ate. If potatoes were a good buy, the school family ate a considerable amount of potatoes. Meals were planned on a day-to-day basis, and it remained for Robinson to institute a weekly menu schedule. The old kitchen in Blake Hall fed about 85 staff and boarding students daily while commuting students were fed a hot lunch (started in 1949) from a separate kitchen.

Total school enrollment was about 300 in 1965 with the boys' dormitory being extremely crowded. Robinson soon insisted that only two students share a room, a policy which caused a slight drop in boarding students. Room, board and tuition were $225 per year, including books. Day students paid tuition of $47 for elementary and $76 for high school. Tuition was still sometimes paid in produce and livestock. Robinson would telephone for the market prices of beef, sheep or produce as needed. After the price had been agreed upon, the books would then indicate a "non cash credit" for the transaction. Somewhere between 50% and 60% of the students annually received some sort of financial aid.[6]

Robinson attributed his easy acceptance as the new mission head to three things. First, during that summer of arrival Dr. Akes and he played on a local all-Hispanic softball team. His two homeruns in the very first game placed him in good standing with the local boys and served to show them that as a Christian he was no sissy. Second, he had done carpentry work all his life and knew construction. Therefore he was able to give meaningful orders and immediately start a preventive maintenance program. Third, coming to McCurdy from a college position put him in good standing with the faculty. McCurdy had always had a reputation as a quality school and Robinson sought to improve it even further.

Fortunately the new superintendent found a dedicated staff awaiting his arrival. Some of the mission workers such as Ada Beringer (1948), Irene Cole (1944) and Avis Williams (1946), had arrived shortly after World War II. Others, such as Ruth Clausius (1952), Enoch and Eustie Rodriguez (1951), Joyce Sass (1955), Ruth Stambach (1952) and Elvira Townsend (1955), had joined the staff during the decade of the 1950s. Still other personnel such as LeVerta Bathke (1963), Maurice and Rhea Bonecutter (1964), Ralph Miller (1962), Roger Odell (1962) and Ernest (1962) and Margie (1964) Sanchez had recently become part of the McCurdy family.

Within the first few years of the new administration Robinson added a number of staff positions. Joining the McCurdy family were Dave and Carol Burgett (1965), Bob and Peggy First (1968), Gerry and Marcia Hunsberger (1966), Don and Mary Hilton (1966), Eloy and Rosina Jacquez (1965), Larry and Sharon Lauber (1966) and Lloyd and Linda Muterspaugh (1966). These staff workers, together with the ones previously mentioned, have been the backbone of the mission in recent years.

One of the first new ventures under the Robinson administration was an outreach to the nearby community through an adult evening school started in 1966. Literally hundreds of Northern New Mexicans took advantage of the opportunity to further their education on the McCurdy campus. There is little doubt that this was one of the thrusts which eventually grew into a technical vocational institute and into the Northern New Mexico Community College a decade later. At the same time, Robinson served on a local committee which programmed a Billy Graham Crusade into the area. The committee was chaired by a Roman Catholic layman and a great deal of ecumenism was experienced.

After careful planning by Robinson and others, McCurdy opened in January 1969 a new type of school for Northern New Mexico, a school of practical nursing. Designed to give further training in the field of medical services, the School of Practical Nursing bridged the gap between the registered nurse and the untrained hospital aide. Hospitals and clinics in Northern New Mexico were crying out for more skilled help and not enough RNs were available.

McCurdy's program was a cooperative effort with the Española Hospital utilizing that facility for on-the-job training. Practical nurses experienced training in laboratory work, X-ray techniques, medical record keeping, physical therapy, medical-surgical techniques, maternal and child care, diet therapy and psychiatric nursing. As the school newsletter stated: "It was another milestone by the staff of the McCurdy School to help the people of the Española Valley help themselves through education."[7]

On November 25, 1969, the first class of Licensed Practical Nurses graduated. The profile of this class is quite revealing. The six proud members of the first class, under Miss Mary Jane Fogal (the Director of Nurses), were Claudia Alexander from Española, a grandmother and member of the Hospital Auxiliary; Clara Gallegos of Guachupanque; Bertha Lopez of Abiquiu, who drove forty miles each way; Mercedes Lucero from Taos, wife of a farmer and mother of seven children ages three to eleven, who traveled some 22,500 miles during the year to pursue her training; Florinda Romero from Truchas (high up in the Sangre de Cristo Mountains), who was a widow with six children; and Linda Romero of the San Juan Indian Pueblo, who worked as an aide at the Española Hospital[8] Surely this is human proof of the tremendous value of such a program.

In 1972 the Director of Nurses left McCurdy to head the Career Ladder Program in Nursing Education for the state. At the same time she served as the President of the New Mexico Nurses' Association. Replacing Fogal was Ruth Hastings, a graduate of the Huron Road School of Nursing in Cleveland, Ohio. As a former Army Nurse with degrees from the University of New Mexico and New Mexico State, she was eminently qualified. Throughout the decade of the 1970s the School of Practical Nursing continued to educate and graduate an average of fifteen to twenty students each year. Frequently the students were married women looking for further education or widows and divorcees seeking employment opportunity. On occasion in recent years several young men entered the school as did several Sikhs from their nearly religious community.

By 1980 it was becoming obvious to McCurdy administrators that something had to be done with this program. It was expensive and McCurdy really did not have adequate laboratory facilities for on-campus work. Also, several nearby colleges, notably the College of Santa Fe, had started similar programs. After an extensive study of needs, financial obligations and alternatives, the difficult decision was reached by McCurdy to merge the school of nursing into the program of Northern New Mexico Community College. After a three year phase-in period. the Community College will be solely responsible for this valuable community outreach.

Another Robinson innovation was the creation of a local School Board of Trustees in 1969. The idea behind this move was to have local input into the decision-making process of the school. Times were changing; the Evangelical United Brethren Church had merged to form the United Methodist Church and the situation of the mission school within the church structure was changed.

Under the former E.U.B. Church, the Board of Missions assumed full responsibility for providing the necessary support. McCurdy was not expected nor was it allowed to seek direct support from individual churches. Under the policy of the new United Methodist Church each institution must seek its own means of support other than through the Board of National Missions. The following quote explains the new church philosophy:

> The strategy of the National Division is to assist in the initiation of mission work wherever it can and in anyway it can with the intention of spinning off that work into local autonomy as fast as it can responsibly do so... The National Division dare not become anchored so that all it can do is support projects launched generations ago...[9]

As admirable and forward looking as this statement might be, it has caused considerable readjustment at the school. In 1969, it appeared to the leaders of the mission that the percentage of support would be reduced each year until it would survive only if local support or other sources were sufficient to sustain it.

Local support in terms of revenue has been difficult to obtain due to the uniqueness of the area. An analysis of this region indicates that state and federal governments own about 80% of Northern New Mexico. This amount includes national forest land, state and national monuments, Bureau of Land Management land and Indian pueblos. There is virtually no local large-scale industry, and unemployment has frequently hit 22% or more. Evidence of the revenue problem is seen by the fact that during the mid-1970s approximately one-third of the population qualified for food stamps.

From 1966 on, the Board of Trustees has been forced to deal annually with financial problems. The Board was first headed by G.K. (Bud) Brasher (1966-70) and then by Dr. Richard Alire (1970-75), both of whom were former McCurdy students. In recent years Española attorney James Thompson (1975-83) and Chimayo businesswoman Florence Jaramillo (1983-   ) have struggled with this on-going financial dilemma.

It is generally recognized that the decade between 1965 and 1975 was a time of dramatic change in American society and it had its impact upon McCurdy. Yet the school prided itself on the consistency of program and Christian witness at a time when there was a great demand to change radically. Sociological changes, new demands on the educational system and an increased enrollment were responded to by changes in programs and an increased staff, yet through it all, traditional values and proven practices were maintained. During this time a development office was established. Thanks chiefly to the efforts of Virgil Hague and Carol Burgett, this office became crucial to the survival of the school.[10]

The fact that the mission school not only survived the difficult early years but actually grew is a miracle in itself. How the mission acquired the very land it rests upon is a story in its own right. In the early years friends and neighbors purchased the land privately and then resold it to the mission. This intermediary action was due to the pressure exerted by the local Roman Catholic Church upon its parishioners not to sell to the Protestants. More than one piece of nearby property was acquired in this manner.

The present football field is located on former Indian land which was purchased by Dr. and Mrs. McCracken and then resold without profit to the school. In this case and in others, school personnel used their own meager funds until such time as the church could reimburse them. The small tract of land where the present bleachers are located was not included in any sale. However, neighbor Yates included it in another sale in 1964 so students would not have to sit on borrowed land for athletic games. In 1970, approxiamtely seventeen acres of orchard land just north of the campus were purchased for the girls dormitory and for future development. Future negotiations will probably involve the sale of several nearby properties privately owned by missionary teachers. Today's campus currently consists of 44 acres of school buildings, playing fields, faculty residences, irrigation ditches and open land.

For those interested in the land purchase history, the following is a brief summary:

1. *Mellie Perkins Tract - August 14, 1915:* Church Erection Society of the Church of the United Brethren in Christ purchased from Miss Perkins the original two-acre tract for $250. It included 205.5 feet of frontage in the San Juan Road and ran westward to the La Lomita irrigation ditch. (Present Blake Hall, Chapel and Administration Building)

2. *Roybal Tract - 1921:* Two acres at a cost of $400. (Present gym, heating plant and laundry)

3. *Murphy Tract - 1925:* Three and one-half acres at a cost of $1. This included 135'5" frontage on San Juan Road (now called Mc-Curdy Road). (Present Superintendent's home, Development office, library and classroom building)

4. *Lujan Tract - 1931:* 4.1 acres at a cost of $380.95. Across the San Juan Road from the original tract. (Present Santa Cruz Church and parsonage)

5. *Herrera and Olivas Tract - 1933:* 1.48 acres at a cost of $170 for pasture and farm buildings. Dairy barn and cattle shelter built here. (Present Student Center)

6. *McCracken Tract - 1940:* Three and one-half acres at a cost of $300. (Present playground space for the elementary school)

7. *Clarence Yates Tract No. 1 - 1943:* One-half acre strip near chapel at a cost of $1,200. (Present clinic and elementary school)

8. *Borrego Orchard Tract - 1946:* 2.42 acres of orchard, gardens and two adobe houses (Present Hyde and Van Essen houses)

Up to this point all the land was purchased through the Home Mission and Church Erection Society of the Church of the United Brethren in Christ.

9. *Martinez Farm Tract - 1955:* 3.15 acres for $1 - good irrigated farm land. (Present "Los Alamos" houses and two mobile homes)

10. *Olivas Orchard Tract - 1961:* 1.37 acres for $1 plus cost. (Present teachers' homes and the garages)

These last two tracts were purchased by the Board of Missions of the Evangelical United Brethren Church.

11. *Mary Walker Property - 1961:* One-sixth acre for $10,000. Contained two buildings. (Present Williams house)

12. *John Yates Tract No. 1 - 1964:* Two large lots 80 x 100 or .36 acres for $1 plus costs.

13. *Clarence Yates Tract No. 2 - 1964:* 1.13 acres with the cost absorbed into the value of houses near clinic, plus a small strip of land near the football field.

14. *John Yates Tract No. 2 - 1965:* .18 acres for two residences. Price absorbed. (Present Burgett and Muterspaugh houses)

These last four purchases were by the Division of Home Missions and Church Extension of the Evangelical United Brethren Church.

15. *John Yates Orchard - 1970:* Approximately 17 acres including the site of the present dormitory. The old Zeigler house was purchased in a separate transaction. The Jake Johnson house was obtained in 1972. This was a special arrangement - partially purchase, partially gift.[1]

The year 1969 appears to have been a banner one for change and creativity at McCurdy. In September, nine United Methodist Churches, the McCurdy Schools, the Española Hospital and the Rio Grande Community Activities formed the Española Valley Group Ministry. The concept of the Group Ministry is that the church assigns ministers to the group, which in turn places them where needed. In this manner a minister can be within the Group Ministry but not have a specific congregation, thus utilizing his talents for all of the churches.

Group Ministry has its own budget and the authority to make decisions. In this manner small churches have the benefit from the knowledge and ability of pastors who, because of their qualities, would normally be assigned to a large congregation. Group Ministry has administered the Counseling Service of Northern New Mexico, which was the outgrowth of Superintendent Robinson's background and concern, and Amigos del Valle, the senior citizens' program. In recent years, Rev. Dennis Heffner, originally from the East Ohio Conference and pastor at the Valley View United Methodist Church in Española, has been the driving force behind the Group Ministry. Several intern pastors from United Methodist theological schools have worked with Group Ministry. An example is Rev. Roger Decker who served in 1980-81 and is now a missionary on the island of St. Martin in the Dutch West Indies.

No mention of Group Ministry can be made without comment on the Española Valley Communities Activities (EVCA). This is another community outreach which originally had its roots with the mission school. Through the sportsmindedness of Rev. Campbell, Robinson and others, a recreation program was started in 1965. Keith Megill, son of a Kansas Evangelical United Brethren minister (his mother had served at McCurdy in 1916-17), was hired by the National Division to head up this new activity. With use of the McCurdy track, McCurdy equipment and college volunteers, Megill created an incredible community-wide outreach.[12]

This model recreation program had hundreds of youths and adults involved in athletics. Megill says that at one time forty-five softball teams were in operation and Española became known as the "Slow Pitch Capital of New Mexico." The local women had twelve teams and won four consecutive New Mexico State championships and competed in four National tournaments.

The result was that by 1973 state newspapers were calling EVCA the most effective recreational program in the state. By the mid-1970s juvenile delinquency was reduced significantly in the Española area of Rio Arriba County. The real value of this outreach, according to Megill, is that Anglos, Indians and Hispanics learned to know each other and love each other. "We came together through athletics - that's been my Christian witness."[13]

In the spring of 1968 the local fire department and the State Department of Health stated that Blake Hall was unsafe for use as a dormitory. The fifty-year-old building had seen heavy use as a dormitory, kitchen and dining room. Plans were made and approved for a new dormitory and a student center. The United Methodist Church approved the project as a recipient of the General Advance Special for 1971-73. An initial goal was set for $100,000 to be raised locally and another $100,000 through foundations and churches. An Española businessman, Don Cimino, headed up the local fund-raising drive, with local pledges eventually going over $100,000. The Albuquerque McCurdy Alumni pledged $5,500, and the Senior Class raised $1,200.[14] Money even came from Africa as the Mutambara, Rhodesian U.M. Church sent $15 in honor of Mrs. Bernice Post, who had served for ten years as a missionary and now worked at McCurdy.[15]

In May 1971, Sam Hollenhead of the National Division arrived on the McCurdy campus to supervise the construction. Hollenhead traveled the country for the National Division building church-related apartments and schools. State-wide publicity was given to McCurdy during the fund-raising efforts as Governor Bruce King proclaimed October 16, 1971 "McCurdy Day" in New Mexico, and locally Mayor Richard Lucero named the week of October 16 as "McCurdy Week" in Española.[16]

The Women's Division of the United Methodist Church approved McCurdy as a project for supplementary giving, with a goal of $50,000 designated for furnishings in the girls' dormitory. An open house was held in the new dormitory on March 12, 1972. The building of 16,912 square feet consisted of 32 student rooms for a total of 64 girls (four girls shared a bath), two apartments for dorm counselors, two patios, two lounges and a chapel. The Student Center consisted of a dining room and kitchen, a snack bar, bookstore, athletic office and several small meeting rooms. The total cost of both projects was $534,000 with the school taking out a construction loan of $380,000. Both buildings were consecrated by Bishop Alsie Carleton of the New Mexico Conference on October 18, 1972.

The two new buildings allowed for record enrollments in both 1972 and 1973. October 1973 found 248 in high school, 124 in junior high, 167 in elementary, 58 at the Alcalde School and 22 in the LPN School, for a record enrollment of 619 students and a staff of 71.[17] Even with the new buildings, this large increase in enrollment meant that there was not enough room for all those wishing to apply. Both parents and the Parish Council of the Holy Cross Church wrote petitions to the United Methodist Church urging them to expand the physical plant and staff. Ernest Sanchez filled a new administrative position and set about organizing the boarding and food services. Sanchez also took over the role of athletic director.

At this point the reader may well wonder what the local Roman Catholic Church was doing with a petition to the United Methodist Church to expand its mission school. Times do change, and one of the changes for the better was the relationship between the local Catholic church and the mission school. As previously mentioned, following years of hostility, feelings slowly improved. McCracken's offer to share the school gym had served well to help heal bad feelings. Following Vatican II there seems to have been a whole new ecumenical effort on behalf of the local Catholic church.

It is necessary for the reader to realize that the priests who, for years, have administered the Holy Cross School and Santa Cruz Catholic Church have come mostly from Spain. Even into the 1970s they have been missionary priests from Spain, not the United States. In any event, in April 1970, the leaders of the Holy Cross School in Santa Cruz and McCurdy leaders approved a plan of cooperation in education aimed at improving the quality of both groups. Under the plan, junior high students would be integrated into two classes for each grade at the McCurdy campus. Further broadening of the junior high curriculum included the classes of industrial arts, home economics, physical education and music. Sister Bernice Garcia taught in McCurdy's religion program using Lutheran materials. Interestingly enough, the Presbyterians also participated in this experiment to a limited degree. Students from the John Hyson Presbyterian School in Chimayo were offered transportation to McCurdy. However, by this time the John Hyson School was beginning to limit the scope of its operation and today has only primary grades.

Surely the move between the Santa Cruz Catholic school and the McCurdy school is unprecedented in the history of both the Catholic and Methodist churches. Obviously others felt that it was an unusual situation also, for in September 1971 a CBS religious news crew from Los Angeles arrived on campus. Bruce C. Mosher of the television and film communications division of the United Methodist Church in New York came to direct the operation. The television film documentary was filmed to show how the United Methodist four-year theme "Reconciliation" was at work. Scenes were shot in McCurdy classrooms, student homes and at the Holy Cross School. Chief participants included Dolph Pringle, Dale Robinson, Glen McCracken, Mary Jane Fogal and Dick Campbell for the school and for the United Methodists. Father Mario Vesqa, Father Archuleta and Sister Bernice Garcia spoke for the Holy Cross School.[18]

The cooperation was exceptional, with the local Catholic church paying a portion of their students' tuition the first year. Local sources indicate that very few problems were experienced during the process. An increased number of Catholic students have remained enrolled at McCurdy, but in recent years the Holy Cross School has reinstituted its junior high grades.[19]

Many and varied are the responsibilities of a mission school. Down through the years student activities have always played an important role in the overall educational goals. Art, band, chorus, drama, industrial arts and athletics have been used as a natural extension of the regularly offered classes, such as English, math, social studies, biology, chemistry, languages, business and religion. Currently there are some seventeen clubs and student activities on campus, ranging from the Chess Club to Los Compañeros, the Spanish Club.

Art has always been an area of importance with McCurdy being one of the few schools in the state in which all grades have a special art program. Under the leadership of Erwin Van Essen a number of special art programs in weaving, pottery and design have been created. Special note cards designed by McCurdy students have made their way through church circles. In 1976 the United Methodist women used art work from McCurdy students for their program resource book.

From the mid-1920s onward McCurdy has gained a reputation as a very athletic-minded school. This was true even when the athletes had to play football on the makeshift field and basketball games were played on an outside court. McCracken, a very sportsminded person, organized the first basketball team before he was officially hired by the school. During his tenure as superintendent (1928-65) he served as president of New Mexico Activities Association (1951-53) and helped to guide that body in its early activities.

Many are the school trophies which line the showcases in the halls of the present student center. In 1936, three trackmen qualified for the State Meet, and in almost every year since 1936 McCurdy has been well represented. In 1957 the school football team placed second in the state, and two of its members made the All-State team. In 1962 the football team garnered the school's first State Championship, winning the Class 'C' competition. The 1965 basketball team was considered outstanding. In 1972 the track team won the district meet, the United Nations Club received special recognition and the chorus received very high ratings. In 1972-73 the basketball team went to the state playoffs with a 21-9 record.

The years 1975 and 1976 were special for McCurdy activities. The basketball team, coached by Enoch Rodriguez, went undefeated in district play and they had the best won-lost record in the state at 26-1. The boys junior varsity basketball team won 44 straight games, six boys made the All-State football team and the football team was named the district champion. In the same year six students made All-State Chorus and one was named a National Merit finalist. Women's liberation hit the McCurdy campus with females being elected President and Vice President of the student body.

The year 1976 continued where the previous year had left off with four students going to State Chorus in February. The boys' basketball team was second in the state and the football team won the State championship. This was the first McCurdy state championship in the 'AA' Class. Head coach Gerald Hunsberger, an Indianian from Taylor University, guided the Bobcats (school nickname) to an 11-1 record. Wins over Laguna-Acoma, Santa Rosa and Ruidoso set up the championship game with Clayton, which was won 22-16. Four players were named to both the UPI and AP All-State teams.

The following year the basketball team with a 23-0 record, again coached by Enoch Rodriguez, placed fourth in the state. The winter of 1978 saw three McCurdy students at the All-State Chorus and a flute player became the first McCurdy student ever to make All-State Band. In 1979, two students made the All-State Concert Band. Other honors found McCurdy students in the string orchestra, the mixed chorus and in the girls chorus. The boys' basketball team was the district champ in 1979, and the football team was again in the state playoffs in 1980 and 1981. The boys' track team placed second in the Class AA State Meet in 1982.

McCurdy experienced a new thrill in 1982 with the first girls' championship in athletics. In recent years, volleyball has taken on a new dimension at McCurdy, culminating in the school's first Girls' State Championship. Coach Sally Shockey, a graduate of Indiana Central, led the girls to a 17-1 season, defeating Moriarty for the Class AA State Volleyball title. Special recognition should go to this team for every girl was a honor roll student. Just to prove that the first title was no accident, the girls repeated the action in 1983. Taking a 20-3 record into the state match, the McCurdy girls defeated Estancia for another championship.

While this is quite a list of accomplishments and honors, the best and most important fact is that McCurdy teams and fans are known throughout the state for their fair play and good sportsmanship. Who says, "Good guys always finish last"? This certainly has not been the case at McCurdy.

Perhaps no one deserves more credit for setting the tone of McCurdy athletics than does José Manuel "Chic" Martinez. Born in Mogote,

Colorado on July 26, 1906, Martinez went to Velarde when it was a boarding school for boys. Part of his annual tuition was paid in potatoes that were sent along to the school on the "Chili Line" (Denver & Rio Grande R.R.). Transferring to McCurdy at Santa Cruz, Chic was a member of the first high school graduating class in 1926.[20]

When Martinez graduated from York College in 1930, bread lines were starting to form across the United States, so he felt fortunate to acquire a teaching job in a small school in Southern Colorado for $60 per month. Chic recalls that sometimes he was paid in paper warrants (vouchers) because there was not enough money for teachers' salaries. Beginning in 1943-44, Martinez taught at McCurdy for several years during the decade of the 1940s. After several years in Nebraska, he returned to the campus in 1953 as a coach and teacher. For most of the next twenty years he was the entire coaching staff responsible for football, basketball and track. Sometimes when there were not enough boys for practice, Martinez and Enoch Rodriguez would suit up for scrimmaging. Martinez's football teams won 96 games and lost only 35 games.[21]

After the arrival of Robinson in 1965, Chic says he received permission to install a water sprinkler system and grass the football field. This made McCurdy's field the first grassed football field in North Central New Mexico. Homecoming on October 3, 1970, saw McCurdy fans honor this man by naming the school football field Martinez Field. Retiring in 1973 after twenty-three and a half years at McCurdy, Chic Martinez epitomizes the Christian philosophy of those many years spent as both a student and teacher at the mission school.

Although sports have always been important at McCurdy, nothing matches the uniqueness of collecting trading stamps and labels. It all started in 1975 when fire damaged the school stationwagon. Betty Smith, the school printer, noticed that the development/printing office closet contained boxes of Betty Crocker labels. She suggested to Superintendent Robinson that he approach the General Mills Co. with the idea that he use labels to purchase a new van to replace the stationwagon. The General Mills folks agreed, and a new McCurdy hobby was created. During the same year the school received enough new spoons for the cafeteria via coupons.[22]

In 1977, Smith read a local news story about a nearby school saving labels from Campbell Soup cans and said to anyone who would listen, "McCurdy can do better." It did! Over 124,000 soup labels were collected for cassette tape recorders, record players and other school equipment.[23] During the same year the school collected 8,745 Post tops which they had redeemed for sports equipment. Apparently the folks at McCurdy were just warming up, for in 1979-80 they accumulated a total of 409,855 labels which were redeemed for valuable school equipment including everything from dictionaries and volleyballs to slide projectors and teaching aids - even a piccolo.[24]

In the spring of 1981, Campbells advertised a one-time-only auction of unusual premiums for Chunky Soup labels. "When we informed the Campbell Soup Co. that our goal for this year's project was to collect a million labels, they thought we were joking." However, by late March the school shipped the company 1,321,975 soup labels - an all-time high. In return McCurdy received a 1981 Dodge twelve-passenger van, a Kimball studio piano and a Texas Instruments computer, with a total value of $14,000.[25]

S&H Green Stamps are the latest project. Between 1978 and 1982 stamp books have brought the school the following: a 59-passenger bus (9,150 books) valued at $18,300; lockers for the girls' dressing room (4,500 books) valued at $9,000; junior high lockers (2,263 books) valued at $9,225. The total savings to the school regarding the Campbell labels, Post tops and S&H stamps is in the vicinity of $100,000.[26]

This collection effort is a team project with the entire McCurdy family as well as United Methodist groups from all over the country participating. What other school in the country has stamp-licking sessions in the school cafeteria? Teachers, students, administrators and volunteers have all aided in this tremendous effort. By all rights this sounds like the end of the story on trading stamps, but it is not. The school has this unique idea that it can replace its old and outdated gymnasium with S&H and other trading stamps. The gym project has already collected over 67,500 books of stamps valued at slightly more than $135,000. The word around McCurdy is "When we reach 100,000 books we will start drawing up the plans." Talk about the "faith of a mustard seed"! In any event, if they succeed the building will probably be called "Licking Gym" with good reason.

Historically one of the most important activities of the educational

118

program at McCurdy is the instruction of religion. Through out the years the mission has dedicated itself to teaching young people that most important ingredient - a faith in Jesus Christ.

Beginning in first grade there are daily reminders. Each elementary class participates in Bible study and has daily devotions in the classroom. Additionally, each class plans and presents a weekly chapel program. By the time a student reaches junior high, he is involved in a religion class as a formal part of his class schedule. The seventh grade students study the New Testament, and the eighth grade students study the Old Testament at least twice a week.

At the high school level each student is required to complete one semester of religion for each year he attends McCurdy. Students may currently choose from one of the following: Drama of the Bible, Four Pictures of Christ (Matthew, Mark, Luke and John), Our Christian Heritage, Liturgy, Comparative Religions, Religion in Literature, Doubt and Faith (a sharing of doubts to bring about new faith), and most recently, Practical Christianity.

Devotions are held each morning over the public address system prior to the start of classes. There are weekly chapel services at all levels, and for boarding students there are devotions before meals. The entire religious focus of the campus is coordinated by a Religious Life Committee composed of both staff and students.

For more than thirty years Ruth Marie Stambach has been a leading spokesperson for the religious aspect of campus life. Coming from York, Pennsylvania, via Lebanon Valley College, Ruth arrived in August 1952. She recalls that in the early 1950s there simply was no communication between the mission school and the nearby Roman Catholic school; however, following Vatican II, relations markedly improved with many Roman Catholic students enrolling at McCurdy. Esther Megill is credited by Stambach as the person responsible for developing a modern religious curriculum so that today a number of religion courses are offered.

Commenting on the current times, Stambach sees students becoming more interested in religious beliefs. For this dedicated worker of the Lord, the real value of McCurdy is in providing the right environment for students to become receptive to religion. God is real in the McCurdy classroom and God is a part of the course of study. Perhaps most important are the many unspoken examples of the staff members twenty-four hours a day as they convey the Christian message in more than just words.[27]

Nowhere has the relationship between religion and education been closer than in the outlying mission or plaza schools. For a number of years these mission schools were operated at Alcalde, Velarde and Vallecitos. Then as both transportation and public schools improved, the need for these schools decreased. One by one each of these outreach schools has been closed; however, the attached churches have remained active. In essence each school was a real neighborhood school and considerable loyalty has been attached to each. Each mission station is in reality its own story. Thus a considerable amount of sadness has followed each school closing.

Velarde, the first mission school opened by Mellie Perkins in 1912, was the first plaza school to close. After trying to hold pre-first and first grade classes only, it became financially necessary to close in 1966. The building continues to be used for community groups such as Head Start and, with aid from the Group Ministry, the church maintains an active congregation.

Georgene McDonald, a former principal at Velarde, exemplifies the dedication of the many teachers who served at Velarde. born in Eugene, Oregon, in 1905, educated at the Universities of Washington and Michigan, McDonald came to New Mexico in 1932. She reports that when she stepped off the train in Lamy, New Mexico, all she could think of was, "I am a stranger in a strange foreign land." Not the type to remain a stranger very long, McDonald served thirty-nine dedicated years at Velarde, Alcalde and Santa Cruz. She retired in 1971.[28]

During the late 1960s, in the mountains fifty miles north of the Mc-Curdy campus, enrollment at the Vallecitos mission school began falling. Actually the community had never recovered economically from the burning of its chief industry, a sawmill, in 1957. With the exception of some hippies in the mid-1960s, the region was just too remote for an increase in population. By 1967, the student enrollment was a mere eight students. So in 1970, a decision was reached to close the school.

Throughout the years the school at Vallecitos had served the community in many ways. It was the chief agent in the community that constantly urged parents to be involved in furthering their children's education. A number of Vallecitos students have gone on to McCurdy High

School, then on to various colleges and professional occupations. Functioning as a health clinic during a typhoid outbreak in the late 1940s, it served the purpose of showing the local people that they could trust the mission for help. For years Dr. Akes and a public health nurse held bimonthly clinics and instructed the community in first aid and health practices at the mission building.

Each of the outlying mission stations has its own people who are special to that particular school and church, and Vallecitos is no exception. Nellwyn Brookhart, born in Decatur, Indiana, in 1921, had dreams of going to Africa. Instead, after three years of study at Ball State, she first arrived at Vallecitos in 1945-46. Recognizing the need for further education, she left for Otterbein College to complete her degree in 1947. It was Nell Brookhart who first told the Pringle family of the needs in northern New Mexico. Returning to the mission field after graduation, Nell taught at Velarde and Santa Cruz. Marrying Max Trujillo, who had been Miss Clippinger's Spanish translator, Nell held down the school position at Vallecitos until its closing in 1970. On loan by the Mission board to the Title I program of the Ojo Caliente School System, Nell keeps the parsonage and church at Vallecitos in fine working condition.[29]

Rev. Adolphus Pringle has made the weekly round trip of 100 miles to Vallecitos for church services for over sixteen years. In addition to serving as the McCurdy Elementary School principal since 1952, Dolph Pringle has served weekends at Wagon Mound for four years and at Tres Piedras for six years. Most recently Dolph serves an outreach congregation meeting in the country club lounge at the Angel Fire Ski Resort near Taos. When one calculates the tremendous distances between these churches and the McCurdy campus (Tres Piedras, 57 miles; Angel Fire, 65 miles one way), one begins to see Rev. Pringle as a modern-day circuit rider and a super salesman for God.

Indeed the Pringles have given much to the New Mexico mission program. Gwen has served as a teacher in home economics and physical education, and for more years than she cares to count she served as faculty sponsor for the cheerleaders. Dolph's sense of humor and love of people is a special gift in itself and his role as elementary principal has kept him in close contact with all phases of the mission work. Through the years the love and dedication of the Pringles have served as a high standard of measure at McCurdy.

The third mission to be opened by Mellie Perkins in 1917 and the last plaza school to be closed was Alcalde. The success of this mission can be measured in many ways, one of which is that in 1947 of the seventy-seven students in the school only seven were Protestant. By 1967 over half of the seventy-two pupils were listed as Protestant.

Many are the dedicated teachers who have served at Alcalde, but perhaps Avis Williams best represents them all. Born in Wisconsin on July 13, 1919, she was educated at Ontario High School and Platteville State College where she received degrees in both elementary and secondary education.[30] Like other eager missionary teachers, she wanted to go overseas (the Philippines was her choice), but World War II interrupted those plans. Arriving in New Mexico in August 1946, Avis was stationed first at Velarde and then transferred to Alcalde. She recalls that few area homes had electricity, some had dirt floors, there were very few cars and washing machines were almost unknown. Her salary was $76 per month plus room and a $15 food allowance.[31]

At Alcalde Avis Williams taught and served as principal for thirty-two years. She credits Georgene McDonald with encouraging her to start a basketball team for the boys. Thus she became the first female basketball coach in all of northern New Mexico. Avis bought the basketballs and uniforms from her own meager funds. Her teams soon won respect because of their fine play. Many are the trophies won by the boys from Alcalde. During the late 1960s, Catholic sisters from their nearby school began attending basketball games at Alcalde Mission, thus opening an improved era of understanding.[32]

Alcalde charged a dollar a month tuition in the 1940s. Students who coud not pay swept floors, cut weeds or did other chores for their payment. The mission school always met the state educational requirements but held longer hours in order to allow for devotions and Bible study. In the early years there was no public school in Alcalde, which is the reason the mission school was opened. However, by the late 1940s, there was a public school across the road and the two were competitive. Williams reports that throughout the decades of the 1940s and 1950s practically every teacher at the local public school was a product of Alcalde Mission and McCurdy. Until the decision of the famous Dixon Case in 1951, the

Catholic sisters were in charge of the public school.[33]

Life was seldom dull at Alcalde, and surely one of the most interesting of the satellite activities of the mission has been the management of La Loma Vista Cemetery. As the only Protestant cemetery in the region, stories involving this burial ground have become a part of the local folklore. Williams says that she had even heard of it in Wisconsin where here church raised funds for its upkeep.[34] Pat (Ashby) Campbell, former teacher at McCurdy and cemetery board secretary, calls it "the cemetery with the most character."[35] It seems that the board was always wrestling with issues such as who was buried where, to whom Dr. McCracken had promised a site but had never written it down, or why new graves which were dug had been previously used. It also seems that new graves would just appear overnight. Even when the gate was locked to control access, people would just climb over the fence and dig a grave anywhere. Avis Williams was startled one day when informed that a priest was officiating in the cemetery - it turned out to be an Episcopalian priest.[36]

Alcalde and the entire Española Valley changed with the construction of Los Alamos (the Atomic City). As the area people found jobs on the hill, new money flowed into Alcalde. Thus transportation improved greatly. With improved roads and improved public schools, enrollment at Alcalde started to decline. From a high of seventy-one students in 1964-65, numbers dropped to forty-one in 1978-79.

Reacting to lower enrollments, higher per-pupil costs and problems meeting the State Fire Code, the McCurdy Board of Trustees voted to close Alcalde with the ending of school on May 23, 1980. Avis Williams transferred her thirty-four years of experience to the McCurdy campus. LaVerta Bathke, of the Minnesota Conference, likewise moved to McCurdy with her seventeen years of experience. Ruth Clausius, the third Alcalde teacher, returned to Wisconsin to care for her ailing parents after twenty-eight years of dedicated service in New Mexico. Although the mission school closed, the Alcalde church has remained open and active and is considered a part of the Española Valley Group Ministry.

In many ways the closing of the outlying plaza schools at Alcalde, Vallecitos and Velarde, as well as the transfer of the school of nursing to the community college illustrates the financial dilemma faced by McCurdy in recent years. Sufficient funding is necessary for the successful operation of any institution and rising costs plus the inflation rate have had their toll on the mission program of the school.

Prior to 1964, McCurdy and other institutions had enjoyed a long period of stable national policies and administration as well as centralized support services. Beginning in 1964, the National Division of the Methodist Church began a process of assessing its relationship to institutions. The same year saw the General Conference restructure the Board of Missions. Even if the 1964 reconstruction had not occurred, there is evidence to indicate that major changes would have occurred with the institutional ministries.[37]

In May 1968, Dr. Ed Carouthers, who was then Associate General Secretary of the National Division, delivered a major address on the subject of church-related institutions. In his speech to the division he spoke of the development policy in the matter of social welfare and health ministries and how compassion can be expressed with the highest resulting facts. He spoke of the tendency of Methodism toward the establishment of ministries of social welfare of various kinds with the accompanying strategy of spinning off as institutional forms into the secular social process wherever and whenever possible. He went on to explain that Methodism has followed a pattern of starting what needs to be started; then it has turned the work over to the community to continue while the church has gone to another place of need to repeat the operation.[38]

By 1979, the church seemed to be asking the question, "Do we see ourselves as providing needed services not provided by the public sector or do we see ourselves providing alternative services?" Obviously the answer to this question and others like it are at the heart of existence for a school like McCurdy. An overriding related fact which is seldom discussed in detail is that the National Division and the church in general do have financial limitations, as each institution does also. Perhaps Lula Garrett of the National Division best summarizes the situation this way:

> Our mandate is unlimited, our resources are limited, and yet we must also respond to the many new needs. That is a dilemma for us, as it is a dilemma for you in local communities as you see a variety of needs around you and you cannot respond to all of them.[39]

An examination of the McCurdy financial picture will show that the school receives three basic types of'financial support: a direct appropriation from the National Division of the Board of Global Ministries of the United Methodist Church; gifts from individuals and churches, sent both directly and through the Advance Special program of the United Methodist Church; and tuition and fees.

Several facts become quickly obvious to anyone studying the figures. First, the direct appropriation from the BOGM is being decreased almost annually as part of the National Division's policy of de-emphasizing institutional programs. Second, the Advance Special money and direct gifts need to be increased as the other appropriation shrinks. Third tuition and fees have increased almost every year and may be reaching the point where lower income and welfare students could be excluded. To date the work-study program of McCurdy has taken care of most of these needs. At the same time the actual cost of educating each student has risen to the point that tuition and fees only account for thirty to thirty-three percent of the real cost. And fourth, scholarship and work aid are available, but this money must come from somewhere, and the twenty-four dollar question of the future will be "Where?"

Through the years McCurdy has received some U.S. Government grant money for such programs as the Right to Read, the nursing school, the Career Ladder, art and music. The high water mark of government grant money was the $21,500 received in 1976. In 1981, through the New Mexico Conference Advance the school received $21, 050 of new money. This increased to $49,475 in 1982, and there are hopes and prayers that this amount from the state churches will grow in the years to come.

In order to secure the future of McCurdy the responsible leaders now recognize the need for new and different sources of revenue. Through increased activity of the Development Office it is hoped that projects such as an Annual Giving Campaign, increased alumni support, corporation or foundation grants, planned giving (wills and bequests) can help to supplement the necessary revenue to continue the worthwhile work being done at McCurdy.

In examining the mission school it is interesting to note that by 1982, the mission had been in continuous operation for seventy years, and yet only four individuals had served as superintendent. These dedicated people have been Miss Lillian Kendig (1918-21); Rev. John Overmiller (1921-

28); Dr. Glen McCracken (1928-65); and Dr. Dale Robinson (1965-82).

Under the leadership of Robinson the school doubled in size, increasing from 300 students in 1965 to an all-time high of 648 by 1977. Two much-needed buildings were completed - the student center and a dormitory. A number of new programs such as the school of nursing, adult education, community recreation and others were put into operation. Naturally the school budget has reflected this increased activity moving upward from $250,000, in 1965-66 to $1,000,000 in 1977-78 and $2,000,000 by 1983-84.

Among staff members, the most appreciated contribution made by Robinson was an improved standard of living. Mission salaries have historically been low, and McCurdy was no exception. In 1965 a new single teacher could expect to start at a salary of $2,600 per year. Married teachers the same year received $3,600, with a maximum salary possible, regardless of longevity, of $4,200. This was certainly not a sufficient income on which to live or raise a family and it certainly was not an equal pay for equal work situation.

Through Robinson's leadership a completely new pay scale was enacted with regular annual increases. By 1977 a starting teacher of any gender could expect an annual salary of $6,180 and could move upward toward a maximum of $11,000. By 1982-83 a teacher with a B.A. degree could begin at $7,512, an M.A. degree could bring in $8,421, and the maximum achievable salary for the longest tenured teachers was moved to $15,240.

Equally important to the welfare of the staff, many of whom have given their entire life's work to the mission was the creation of an adequate retirement plan through TIAA/CREF. A tax-sheltered annuity plan was started for those desiring it, and an improved health and accident policy was instituted through the Minister's Life Insurance Company. In addition to the cash salary, a house or apartment and utilities were provided on campus whenever possible. Approxiamtely three-fourths of the staff do live on the campus. If campus housing is available or if the staff member chooses, a cash housing allowance is made. Allowances were instituted in 1970 $1,200 per year and increased several times to the current level of $2,400. The concept of the cash allowance is to allow the teachers the opportunity of owning their own homes. A number of teachers have moved off the campus and have become active in various phases of community life, thus being a Christian witness to different neighborhoods.

The management of a mission school is a difficult position, and unfortunately, Robinsoin's health began to fail. After sixteen years of service and a one year leave of absence, Robinson resigned his position as superintendent. Named to guide the reins of McCurdy's mission program was David S. Burgett. Son of missionary parents, Burgett was reared in Pennsylvania and Kentucky. Graduating from the Red Bird Mission High School, Burgett received a B.S. degree from Eastern Kentucky State University in 1953. While teaching in the Illinois public schools, he received a Master of Education degree from the University of Illinois in 1958. Moving to the McCurdy campus in 1965, the Burgett family (wife Carol, sons Kevin and Tim and daughter Julie) have been involved in all phases of school and church life. Burgett served as the McCurdy High School principal from 1967 to his appointment as superintendent.

Other changes in 1982-83 saw long-time teacher Linda Muterspaugh named high school principal. Indiana Central graduates Lloyd and Linda Muterspaugh have served McCurdy since 1966. After almost fifteen years of service, in retirement no less, business manager Robert First resigned. Replacing First at the financial desk was Everett Matzigkeit, with twenty years of experience as a missionary in Zimbabwe with the World Division of the Board of Global Ministries.

In his first message as the new superintendent Burgett told mission supporters:

> McCurdy continues as an educational institution in Christian mission, dedicated to the development of young people in the name and image of Jesus Christ. Our Christian community is the mode by which we achieve this purpose. We could not fulfill our mission except in this context. It is only by God's grace that we as students and staff live and work in this setting. It is not by our own words and deeds but by God's direction that we continue the long tradition that is McCurdy.[40]

Much as been accomplished in the past and much still needs to be done. The struggle has never been easy. The region served by the mission is remote and vast and some villages are isolated. The population, though growing, is still small and widely scattered. The land is arid, and irrigation is still necessary. Economically the region has improved, but the lack of an industrial base and the acreage owned by the various government agencies still result in a very low tax base. High unemployment in many of the outlying communities is still a way of life. The local public schools have improved over the years but still face many problems. Local politicians still determine the policy and in many cases do the actual hiring and firing of school employees. McCurdy - as well as the public schools - is faced with students who struggle with family break-ups, increased use and misuse of aclohol, drugs and sex, lack of an authority figure in the home, lack of self-discipline, parental rejection and a feeling of little self-worth.

There is an old proverb which says, "Those who want to leave an impression for one year should plant corn; those who want to leave an impression for 100 years should educate a human being." McCurdy is dedicated to providing that impression in the name and spirit of our Lord Jesus Christ.[41]

In this modern age the McCurdy Mission School still provides a high-quality educational program in a Christian environment. As in the past, today McCurdy Mission School encourages each student to understand and accept himself as well as to appreciate those from various backgrounds.

McCurdy continues to be an instrument for change in the region. Like a bright and powerful beacon, the mission still sends out God's light throughout the Española Valley.

NOTES

[1] Interview with Dr. Dale E. Robinson, Española, New Mexico, May 15, 1981.

[2] Interview with Dr. Robinson

[3] Interview with Mrs. Margaret Robinson, Española, New Mexico, July 7, 1982.

[4] Interview with Dr. Robinson

[5] Interview with Dr. Robinson

[6] Interview with Dr. Robinson

[7] The McCurdy School Newsletter, December 1962, p. 2.

[8] The McCurdy School Newsletter, December 1962, p. 2.

[9] The McCurdy School Newsletter, December 1969, pp. 1, 4.

[10] Correspondence with David S. Burgett, Española, New Mexico, November 1, 1983.

[11] *Valuation of Mission Properties*, Division of National Missions, Evangelical United Brethren Church, January 1968 and other sources.

[12] Interview with Keith Megill, Española, New Mexico, July 12, 1982.

[13] Interview with Keith Megill.

[14] *McCurdy Message*, November 1971, pp. 1-2.

[15] *McCurdy Message*, August 1972, p. 1.

[16] *McCurdy Message*, November 1971, pp. 1-2.

[17] *McCurdy Message*, October 1973, p. 1.

[18] Sound Track from *Lamp Unto My Feet*, CBS News Film, 1972.

[19] Interview with Miss Elvira Townsend and Erwin Van Essen, Española, New Mexico, July 10, 1983. It is interesting to note that prior to 1968 the percentage of students listed as Roman Catholic at McCurdy was usually 10%. By 1977-78 this figure changed to 55%.

[20] Interview with Jose M. Martinez, Antonito, Colorado, May 11, 1981.

[21] Interview with Jose M. Martinez.

[22] Interview with Mrs. Betty Smith, Española. New Mexico, July 11, 1983.

[23] Interview with Mrs. Betty Smith.

[24] *McCurdy Message*, May 1978, p. 1.

[25] *School Records*, unpublished papers from the Development Office, April 6, 1982.

[26] *School Records*.

[27] Interview with Ruth Marie Stambach, Española, New Mexico, May 13, 1981.

[28] Interview with Georgene McDonald, Española, New Mexico, May 13, 1981.

[29] Interview with Mrs. Nellwyn Brookhart Trujillo, Vallecitos, New Mexico, June 30, 1983.

[30] Interview with Avis Williams, Española, New Mexico, May 11, 1981.

[31] Interview with Avis Williams.

[32] Interview with Avis Williams.

[33] Interview with Avis Williams.

[34] Interview with Avis Williams.

[35] Correspondence with Mrs. Patricia Campbell, El Paso, Texas, April 10, 1981.

[36] Interview with Avis Williams.

[37] Transcription of Lula M. Garrett's speech to the Agency Cluster meeting in Arlington, Texas, February 23-24, 1979, pp. 1-2.

[38] Dr. Ed Carouther's address to the National Division quoted by Lula M. Garrett's speech to the Agency Cluster in Arlington, Texas, February 23-24, 1979, Transcription, pp. 2-3.

[39] Lula M. Garrett, p. 8.

[40] *McCurdy Message*, September-October 1982, p. 2.

[41] *McCurdy Message*, January 1974, p. 2.

IMPORTANT DATES AND EVENTS IN
THE HISTORY OF THE McCURDY MISSION SCHOOLS

1910 Rev. Schlotterbeck visited Upper Rio Grande Valley.
Mellie Perkins volunteered to start a mission school.

1911 Mellie Perkins studied at Campbell College with Edith McCurdy.

1912 Mellie Perkins and student helper Susanita Martinez arrived in Velarde to start the first school.

1914 Bessie Haffner, second teacher, arrived at Velarde.

1915 School moved to Santa Cruz and the original building was dedicated as "The Edith McCurdy Mission."

1916–17 Bibles and other Protestant materials burned by priests in Velarde and Santa Cruz Plaza.

1917 Chapel building with two classrooms dedicated.
New school started at Alcalde.

1918 Mellie Perkins left New Mexico.
Lillian Kendig appointed principal.

1919 Both boys and girls housed at Santa Cruz.

1920 First eighth grade graduation.

1921 Rev. & Mrs. Overmiller arrived to assume duties at the Mission.
New girls dormitory dedicated (later named Blake Hall).

1922 First high school classes offered.

1925 Basketball team organized by McCracken.

1926 First high school class graduated.
Football team organized by Overmiller.

1927 School building constructed at Velarde.

1928 Overmiller left the Mission and McCracken became Superintendent.

1930 School and church started at Vallecitos.

1931 McCurdy gymnasium burned before total completion.

1937 Church and school building dedicated at Vallecitos.

1940 Rebuilt gym dedicated and named for Glen McCracken.

1941 Health work begun; first nurse arrived.

1942 Industrial arts building completed.
Outreaches to Ojo Caliente, La Madera, Petaca and others begun.

1943 Teachers' cottage built at Alcalde.

1944 McCurdy Medical Clinic begun.

1945 Present superintendent's home built at McCurdy.

1946 Merger of Evangelical and United Brethren Church.
New clinic constructed. Santa Cruz parsonage built.

131

1948   First four rooms of McCurdy Elementary built.
        Española Hospital constructed and dedicated.
1950   Laundry, Pasteurizer and central heating building constructed.
        Boys' dormitory completed (now called Bachman Hall).
        Petaca Church dedicated.
1952   Administration building built.
        Regular church service started at Tres Piedras.
1953   Santa Cruz Church built and dedicated.
1955   North Central accreditation of high school.
1957   Hernandez congregation organized.
1962   McCurdy Elementary dedicated. New women teachers' cottage built.
        Football State Championship.
1963   Santa Cruz Church Fellowship Hall built.
1964   Additions made to dormitory, gym and kitchen.
        New church completed at Hernandez.
1965   McCracken retired; Robinson arrived to become Superintendent.
        Farm program phased out.
        Española Valley Community activities begun.
1966   Local Board of Trustees formed. Velarde Mission School closed.
        Church and community activities continue.
1967   North Central accreditation reaffirmed.
1968   Merger of E.U.B. and Methodist churches to form the United
        Methodist Church.
        McCurdy School placed under Board of National Missions.
1969   School of Practical Nursing begun in old clinic building.
        Beginning of McCurdy Schools Newsletter.
1970   Vallecitos Mission School closed. Church and community activities
        continue.
        Seventh and eighth graders from Holy Cross enrolled at McCurdy.
        Football field named Martinez Field for J.M. "Chic" Martinez.
1971   CBS television crew filmed *A Lamp Unto My Feet*.
        Local fund raising netted more than $100,000 for new girls' dormitory.
1972   Student Center completed. Jake Johnson property annexed.
        "Open House" at new girls' dormitory (named for Catherine Ross
        Pilling).
1974   Van purchased with Betty Crocker coupons.
        North Central accreditation reaffirmed.
1975   Bleachers and scoreboard added to the football field.
1976   Considerable remodeling of buildings. Football State championship.
        Summer Work Camps reorganized by Rev. Marks.

1977 Half million Campbell Soup labels collected for A/V and playground equipment.
Budget of $1,000,000 reached.

1980 Alcalde Mission School closed; church continues.
New school bus purchased with Green Stamps.
Studio piano and computer purchased with soup labels.

1981 Blake Hall remodeled.
North Central accreditation reaffirmed.

1982 Nursing program merged with Northern New Mexico community College.
Girls won State Volleyball Championship.

1983 Robinson resigned due to health;
David Burgett named Superintendent.
Girls won 2nd State Volleyball Championship.

PASTORS AND McCURDY MISSION SCHOOL WORKERS
1912 – 1983

1959-62 ACKLEY, REV. & MRS. OWEN

1951– AKES, DR. LEONARD

1983-84 ALLEN, CRAIG

1927-29 ALLEN, MR. & MRS.

1972– ALLISON, KATIE

1982– AMADOR, MABLE

1964-65 ANDERSON, KEN

1970-71 APODACA, RITA

1973– ARCHULETA, LEVILA

1980– ARELLANO, LEVY

1970-82 ASHBY, PATRICIA

1983– ATENCIO, SAM

1952-54 ATENCIO, TOBY V.

1937-38 BABLER, VIOLA

1929-51 BACHMAN, IRENE

1980– BAKER, GRACE

1943-56 BALL, HELEN

1970-76 BARBER, REV. & MRS. ED

1980-81 BARTON, MARY

1963-81 BATHKE, LAVERTA

1952-54 BEASLEY, GERTRUDE

1943-45 BEASON, EVELYN

1977-79 BECKER, MELVIN

1971-73 BECKMAN, MR. & MRS. GEORGE

1981 BEESLEY, KENNETH

1951-53 BELL, REV. & MRS. RAY
56–58, 70–78

1922-23 BENNER, MARY

1948– BERINGER, ADA

1966-67 BIDDLE, ODESSER
70–73, 74–

1961-62 BIZEL, JETHRO

1922-56 BLAKE, LENA

1956-58 BOCKENHAUER, RAMONA

1964– BONECUTTER, REV. & MRS. M.

1963-65 BOUQUIN, JESSIE

1953-59 BOWERS, MR. & MRS. WILFRED

1936-44 BOWERSOX, EDNA
47–48

1969-76 BOYLE, MARTHA

1939-40 BRADLEY, CHARLENE

1975-77 BRANCH, LOUISA

1941-46 BRANDSTETTER, REV. A.L. & GRACE
50–52

1929-33 BRANDSTETTER, WILMA

1915-25 BRAWNER, MARY

1977-82 BREWER, MR. & MRS. RONALD

1929-31 BROOKS, SARAH

1980-81 BROWN, REV. & MRS. BOB

1952-53 BROWN, DORIS

1970-80 BROWN, JENNIE

1951-52 BROWN, MR. & MRS. LEWIS

1958-60 BROWN, LILLIE
64–

1963-67 BROWN, ORLANDO

1973-84 BROWN, VIVIAN

1965– BURGETT, MR. & MRS. DAVID

1982– BUSTOS, ROBERTA

1959-63 BURKETT, MARY LOU
65–71

1947-61 BUTTERWICK, HELEN

1937-38 CALDWELL, EVALINA

1937-40 CALDWELL, REV. & MRS. I.E.

1961-78 CAMPBELL, REV. RICHARD C.

1961-67 CAMPBELL, FLORENCE

1964-65 CAPERTON, BEVERLY

1935-43 CARPENTER, REV. & MRS. R.

1970-72 CHAPMAN, RUTH

1932-33 CHAVEZ, GUILLERMA

1928-29 CLARK, MR. & MRS. JESS

1952-79 CLAUSIUS, RUTH

1920-47 CLIPPINGER, LULA M.

1967-69 COATES, RETTA

1941-42 COBE, JARVIS

1948-50 COLDRON, VIRGINIA

1944-60 COLE, IRENE
63–

1965-68 COMBS, MARY

1974– COOPER, JOYCE

1938-41 CORBIN, MR. & MRS. L. WAYNE
46–51

1980– CORDOVA, SYLVIA

1958-62 CRAWFORD, BERYL

1961-63 CURTIS, MR. & MRS. TED

1926–27 CUSIC, MR. & MRS. CHARLES
1933–34 DAGGETT, MRS. G.
1945–47 DAVIS, ADELLE
1980–81 DECKER, REV. & MRS. RODGER
1967 DELGADO, SARAH
1979–82 DENIPAH, NATALIE
2954–55 DENNY, MRS. OTIS
57–58
1950–51 DICKERSON, ELOISE
1950–55 DIVINE, JOSSIE
1927–28 DODSON, MRS.
1976–80 DOMINGUEZ, MAGGIE
1983– DOMINGUEZ, PETE
1982– DOMINGUEZ, ROSA
1971–77 DOYLE, JUDITH
1978– DRURY, MARGARETTA
1974 DURAN, ELONARD
1976–77 DURAN, MARGIE
1919–21 DYE, REV. & MRS. W.E.
1982–83 EASLEY, REBECCA
2976–77 EASTMAN, LINDA
1943–44 EIMBRINK, ZELDA
1982– ELTZROTH, KERRY
1920–21 EMERICK, SARAH
1942–43 ENGLE, NELL
1966–68 EVANS, REID
1950–52 EVELAND, LUTHERIA
1972–74 FALDE, CAROL
1982– FEEBACK, NANCY
1947–49 FELLERS, MR. & MRS. I.C.
1969–71 FELTS, CHARLES
1972–73 FERRELL, REV. GENE
1963–65 FIEGEL, RUTH
1970–79 FIRST, PEGGY
1968–83 FIRST, ROBERT
1969–73 FISHER, LYNDALL
1968–72 FOGAL, MARY JANE
1960–67 FRANK, VIRGINIA
1968–67 FREDRICK, REV. & MRS. E.
1936–38 FRESHLEY, ELNORA
1934–39 FRESHLEY, HAROLD
1924–26 FRIEZE, RUTH
1953–56 GABEL, EVELYN
64–70
1968–74 GALLEGOS, CELESTINO
1978– GALLEGOS, JOYCE

1971–72 GALLEGOS, PAUL
1970–72 GARCIA, SISTER BERNICE
1976– GARCIA, ERMENY
1967– GARCIA, GLORINDA
1979– GARCIA, RENEE
1974–75 GARCIA, THERESA
1981–83 GARCIA, TONITA
1944–48 GARLOCK, LORRAINE
1964–71 GERRISH, WILLIAM
1948–49 GILBERT, CLARA
1970 GILL, MRS. JOHN A.
1969–70 GIRON, CLAUDIA
1927–29 GISH, REV. & MRS. C.C.
1965–66 GLASER, REV. & MRS. W.K.
67–78
1982–83 GOMEZ, ROBERT
1955–57 GONZALES, GREGORIO
1948–50 GOODRICH, EUNICE
1976–82 GOULD, CHARLOTTE
1981– GRAVES, REV. & MRS. ELLIOTT
1960–62 GREEN, MR. & MRS. LAWRENCE
1979–80 GRIEGO, GEORGE
1976–77 GRIEGO, PEDRO
1919–20 GRIGGS, DR. ZENORA
1946–47 GUILD, PAULINE
1913–16 HAFFNER, BESSIE
1969–71 HAGER, MARJORIE
1970–83 HAGUE, DR. & MRS. VIRGIL
1979–80 HAGUE, JIM
1981–82 HAIRSTON, ELIZABETH
1943–47 HALL, HELEN (AKES)
1928–30 HAMAKER, GERTRUDE
1918–22 HARDY, ANNA
1940–42 HARDY, ELVA
1939–41 HARRIS, NORMA
1972–82 HASTINGS, RUTH
1927–28 HAWKINS, MRS.
1970–79 HAYES, MR. & MRS. PAUL
1972–77 HAYNES, TOM
81–
1947–48 HECKMAN, MARY
1971–72 HEFFNER, REV. & MRS. DENNIS
75–
1976–81 HEILMAN, GERALDINE
1955–57 HEISEY, MIRIAM
1946–47 HEMBREE, MITTIE

1980–81 HEMSWORTH, JIM
1964–67 HENDRIX, MR. & MRS. MARVIN
1970–74 HERRERA, MR. & MRS. R.B.
1979–   HERRERA, ROSS
1923–29 HERRICK, DELIA
30–59
1927–29 HERRICK, LOWELL
1922–29 HERRICK, VERA
33–37, 42–43
1923–29 HERRICK, ZELLA
30–63
1938–40 HIATT, MR. & MRS. HERBERT
1966–   HILTON, MR. & MRS. DON
1955–56 HIMES, MR. & MRS. M.
1965–67 HOLCOMB, CLARA
1983–   HOLLEY, GREG
1942–43 HOLLIS, AMANDA
1948–50 HOLMAN, DOROTHY
1953–55 HORNBAKER, REV. ROBERT
1973–76 HORNSBY, MR. & MRS. STAN
1942–49 HORST, CORA
1962–71 HOUMES, JANET
1918–19 HOUSEKEEPER, DORA
1925–26 HOWE, MR. & MRS. JOSEPH
1978–79 HUBER, REV. JEROME
1949–51 HUFF, FRED
1952–53 HUGHES, MARY ELLEN
1974–76 HUGHEY, BILL
1966–   HUNSBERGER, MR. & MRS. G.
1972–   HYDE, BETH
1951–52 IRWIN, GOLDIE
1974–75 JACKSON, DAVIS
1979–   JACOBS, JOYCE
1965–   JACQUEZ, ELOY
1970–73 JACQUEZ, ROSINA
1965–66 JAMES, SHARNA
1973–79 JANNEY, TRUDY
1936–38 JARAMILLO, ELACIO
1947–49 JARAMILLO, CLADYS
1931–34 JEFFERS, HAROLD
1933–35 JEFFORDS, PEARL
1954–56 JEFFRIES, COMMIE
1981–   JIMENEZ, CECILIA
1965–67 JIVIDEN, JOYCE
1981–82 JOHNSON, KAY
1972–77 JOHNSON, MR. & MRS. W.W.

1954–59 JORDAN, REV. & MRS. ANDY
1958–59 JORDAN, MR. & MRS. ROBERT
1945–49 KECK, EMILY
1924–28 KEESEY, HAZEL
1950–51 KEIL, GEORGE
1971–72 KELLER, WILLIAM
1968–74 KELLEY, ANN
1916–25 KENDIG, LILLIAN (COLE)
1947–48 KESSEL, HAVEN
1952–53 KINDRED, JAMES
1918   KING, CALLIE
1965–65 KINSEY, HELEN
1954–57 KLINGER, JOAN
1968–69 KLUMP, VIRGIL
1929–33 KNEALE, EFFIE
1959–60 KUHN, RICHARD
1921–22 LaFEVER, MAUDE
1930–39 LANGDON, MARIE
1967–69 LANGE, REV. & MRS. DONALD
1953–55 LARSON, REV. ANDREW
1972–73 LATTA, LINDA
1966–   LAUBER, MR. & MRS. LAWRENCE
1973   LIFE, REV. & MRS. LAWRENCE
1978–79 LINDSLEY, MARJORIE
1927–28 LOBB, REV. WALTER
1977–78 LOPEZ, DELFINO
1968   LOPEZ, SUSIE
1966–71 LORD, JEANNE M.
1949–53 LORENZ, MR. & MRS. JIM
1924–26 LOVE, REV. & MRS. J.R.
1973–74 LOVEKIN, JOAN
1980–83 LUCERO, RUBEN, JR.
1916–19 LUCKEY, LELA
1947–48 LUNA, SARA
1972–73 MAESTAS, MARY
1957–65 MAHOOD, MARIE
1916–17 MARKAY, LILLIAN
1976–   MARKS, REV. DOUGLAS
1977–   MARNER, DORIS
1980–   MARQUEZ, JENNY
1948–49 MARSHALL, BEULAH
1946–47 MARTIN, EILEEN
1978–81 MARTIN, DR. & MRS. WILLIAM
1977   MARTINEZ, BEN
1983   MARTINEZ, CAROLYN

1978   MARTINEZ, GEORGE
1943-44 MARTINEZ, MR. & MRS. J.M.
46-50, 53-73
1977-81 MARTINEZ, KENNETH
1977-   MARTINEZ, MARIAN
1081-83 MARTINEZ, MARY ANN
1980-   MARTINEZ, MIKE
1942-43 MARTINEZ, MRS. NICK
1930-37 MARTINEZ, NICOLASSA FRESHLEY
1961-63 MARTINEZ, ROMAN
1916-17 MARTINEZ, SUSANITA
1974-   MARTINEZ, MR. & MRS. SIXTO
1979-81 MARTINEZ, VICTOR
1982-   MATZIGKEIT, MR. & MRS. E.
1981-83 McCAULEY, MARY
1954-56 McCLARREN, LLOYD
1926-65 McCRACKEN, DR. GLEN F.
1922-65 McCRACKEN, VIOLET
1932-71 McDONALD, GEORGENE
1945-50 McFARLAND, REV. & MRS. PAUL
1952-53 McKOWN, JOHN
1952-55 McPHERSON, MRS. HAROLD
1931-35 MEDINA, MR. & MRS. C.E.
51-64
1966-68 MEGILL, ESTHER
1965-81 MEGILL, KEITH
1973-76 MENEFEE, REV. LAWRENCE
1957-59 MEYER, DORIS JEAN
1935-36 MIDDLETON, MAXWELL
1962-64 MILHOUSE, PAULINE
1954-55 MILLER, ALMA
1964-65 MILLER, CAROL
1947-48 MILLER, DOROTHY
1967-70 MILLER, ELIZABETH
1940-42 MILLER, LOIS
1973-76 MILLER, PATRICIA
1962-65 MILLER, REV. RALPH
70-
1949-65 MILLION, ROSE
1969-72 MIRANDA, ELSIE
1972-73 MITCHELL, MABLE
1969-71 MOE, DONALD
72-73
1973-74 MOE, SOPHIE
1943-47 MOFFAT, LILLIAN
1968-70 MONDRAGON, ANTONIA

1968-74 MONTOYA, ELIRIA
1977-82 MONTOYA, JOAN
1981   MONTOYA, ROY
1915-16 MOORE, IRMA
1973-80 MOORE, BONNIE
1944-46 MORTON, MR. & MRS. HOWARD
1973-83 MOUNTAIN, ALMA
1970-72 MUÑOZ, JOHN
1965-66 MURPHY, MR. & MRS. OLA
1966-   MUTERSPAUGH, MR. & MRS. LLOYD
1981-83 MUTZ, HOYT
1955-56 NAFE, JANET
1923-24 NALEY, MRS.
1929-33 NEAL, MARY
1959-63 NEHRING, ROBERT
64-67
1965-67 NELSON, DIXIE
1962-65 NEWELL, ANNA
1922-35 NEWMAN, CORA
1918   NEWMAN, LOTTIE
1967-69 NISWENDER, MARGARET
1951-56 NOBLE, RUTH
1938-39 NORRIS, JANE
1972-73 NOVAKOSKI, SISTER MARY
1962-   ODELL, MR. & MRS. ROGER
1957-74 OLIVAS, MR. J.M.
1962-63 ONEY, BURLAH ANN
1968-69 ORTEGA, ERNESTINA
1921-28 OVERMILLER, REV. & MRS. J.R.
1961   OVERTON, LENORA
1964-65 PADEN, KATHRYN
1912-18 PERKINS, MELLIE
1951-53 PETERS, JUSTINA
1943-43 PETERSON, MATHILDE
46-55
1929-31 PHILIPPI, MR. & MRS. C.B.
1969-77 PIMBLEY, PATRICIA
1933-34 POCOCK, FLORENCE
1961-67 POMEROY, FRED
1962-67 POMEROY, SANDRA
1967-68 POMEROY, RON
1922-24 POTTS, ETHEL
1981-82 PRESTON, MARSHA
1947-   PRINGLE, REV. A.W.
1947-81 PRINGLE, GWENETH
1976-77 PRINGLE, MR. & MRS. JOSEPH

1930–31 PROCTOR, EDNA
1957–67 PRUETT, ETHEL
1982– QUELLE, MARGARET
1976 QUINTANA, ARTHUR
1977–78 QUINTANA, URBAN
1924–26 RASOR, FREDA
1972–73 RAYBURN, BONNIE
1964–65 REAGLE, LENA
1981 REID, DONALD
1981– REID, REV. HOMER
1973–80 REIN, SERENE
1963–64 RICE, JACK
1974–76 RIVERA, ROSIE
1934–35 ROBERTS, MR. & MRS. ALVIN
1954–55 ROBERTSON, MR.
1965–83 ROBINSON, DR. & MRS. DALE
1951– RODRIGUEZ, MR. & MRS. ENOCH
1973– RODRIGUEZ, RUBY
1915–16 ROMERO, ANGELICA
1980– ROMERO, MARY LOUISE
1978– ROMERO, TEOFISTA
1967–78 ROMERO, VIOLA
1940–41 ROWE, T.T.
1973–74 ROYBAL, BARBARA
1979–83 ROYBAL, DAVID
1969 ROYBAL, VIOLETA
1955–58 RUYBALID, MR. & MRS. R.
1941–43 SALAZAR, BERNARDINO
1983– SALISBURY, MR. & MRS. JOEL
1983– SANCHEZ, ANITA
1952–65 SANCHEZ, MR. & MRS. A.
1962– SANCHEZ, ERNESTO
1964– SANCHEZ, MARGIE K.
1957–71 SANCHEZ, MR. & MRS. FRANKLIN
1957–59 SANCHEZ, REV. & MRS. H.
62–69
1974–77 SANCHEZ, KAY
1973– SANCHEZ, LYDIA
1981– SANCHEZ, PHILLIP
1947–54 SANDERS, CHARLENE
1967–68 SANDOVAL, EZEQUIEL
1968–70 SANDOVAL, LUIS
1955–61 SASS, JOYCE
63–
1941–43 SCHAFER, ANNA
1965–68 SCHATTSCHNEIDER, MR. & MRS. E.

1975–76 SCHATTSCHNEIDER, WILLIAM
1933–35 SHEAFFER, REV. ELEANOR
1959–61 SCHENDEL, MERLIN
1933–28 SCHLOTTERBECK, REV. C.A.
1963–64 SEARCY, JEAN
1941–45 SEARS, MR. & MRS. ALDEN B.
1917–18 SHANKLIN, ELLA
1959–60 SHELTON, PEGGY
1931–34 SHILLING, MR. & MRS. FRED
1976– SHOCKEY, SALLY
1972–76 SHOCKEY, SUSAN
1950–51 SIEWERT, MILTON
1978–79 SINGH, DON
1976–77 SLOAN, SEAGLE
1919 SLOAT, CARRIE
1966–69 SMITH, MR. & MRS. ARTHUR
1978– SMITH, BEN
1973– SMITH, BETTY
1974–75 SMITH, JAN
1974–77 SMITH, REV. & MRS. LeGRAND
1918–22 SMITH, RUTH
1961–62 SNIDER, CAROLYN
1957–59 SNYDER, LYMAN
1976–80 SNYDER, SHARON ALLEN
83–84
1980– SOMMER, ENOYSE
1954–55 SOVIAK, MR.
1952– STAMBACH, RUTH
1982– STAMETS, STEPHAN
1951–55 STENZEL, EDITH
1968–78 STEVENSON, MR. J.M.
1977–80 STRUTHERS, CAROL
1956–76 SUAZO, MR. & MRS. ALFREDO
1956–57 SUAZO, MRS. VICTOR
1968–70 SUNDERMANN, CARLOS
1927–28 SVETLIKIK, MARY
1962–70 SYNSTEGARD, FERN
1940–43 TACK, MELVA
1956–61 TATE, LOUISE
1956–57 TAYLOR, VERA
1959–61 TEMPLETON, REV. & MRS. R.
1979–80 TEMPLETON, ROBERT
1920–21 TESTERMAN, PEARL MEGILL
1978–79 THACKABERRY, MARY
1978– THOMAS, JOHN

1972–   THOMPSON, MR. & MRS. BRIAN
1949–51 TITTLE, LYLA
1943–45 TOMLINSON, KATHLEEN
1955–   TOWNSEND, ELVIRA
1977–78 TRICKEY, LYNN
1954–55 TRUESDALE, WYLMA
1956–62 TRUJILLO, AMADA
1981   TRUJILLO, CHARLENE
1977–78 TRUJILLO, FREDDIE
1981   TRUJILLO, IGNACIO
1945–46 TRUJILLO, NELLWYN
48–
1975–80 TRUJILLO, TINA
1974–78 TUNNELL, RON
1956–70 VALDEZ, EMMA
1979   VALDEZ, NELSON
1969–70 VALDEZ, RICHARD
1976–77 VALENCIA, PEDRO
1959–   VAN ESSEN, ERWIN
1949–50 VARCE, PAULINE
1963   VARNER, MR. L.L.
1956–58 VASQUEZ, IDA
62–64
1944–47 VERMILLION, LILLIAN
1968–73 VICKER, MR. & MRS. WILLIAM
1967–68 VIGIL, ANTONITA
1971–73 VIGIL, DORA
1926–27 WALBORN, CONSTANCE
1943–49 WALKER, REV. HAYES
1943–58 WALKER, MRS. HAYES
1949–51 WALLACE, MAE
1963–64 WALLWORK, BETTY
1978–   WARDEN, REV. & MRS. DAVID
1941–47 WARNER, MARY LUE
1926–30 WARREN, FLORENCE
1920–22 WATTS, MATIE
1945–46 WERTZ, BLANCHE
1948–50 WEST, MR. & MRS. LEON
1929–30 WHITE, MYRTLE
1982   WICKERSHAM, DANIEL
1980–   WICKERSHAM, MARGARET
1969–70 WILLARD, RUTH
1950–53 WILLEMS, REV. & MRS. ISAAC
1919–28 WILLHIDE, BESSIE
1930
1946–   WILLIAMS, AVIS

1939–40 WOLF, CLARENCE
1939–45 WOLFORD, PEARL
1918–24 WOLHEITER, BERTHA
1979–83 WOOD, BOB
1979–80 WOOD, YVONNE
1927–31 WRYE, WHRELDA, J.
1931–32 YORK, REV. & MRS. WILBUR
1946–54 YOUNG, REV. & MRS. WILLIAM
66–67
1948–51 ZAHN, RUTH
1946–76 ZIEGLER, DR. & MRS. S.R.

PERSONS WHO HAVE GIVEN TIME AS VOLUNTEER WORKERS

ABSHIRE, HELEN
ACKERMAN, MR. & MRS. CLIFTON
AKES, VERNON
ALLEN, CRAIG
ARBOGAST, MR. & MRS. PAIGE
BEARD, MR. & MRS. LEE
BEEBE, MR.& MRS. JACK
BEEBOUT, HOWARD
BERG, MR. & MRS. FRED
BETHEL, MR. & MRS. EMERY
BOLINGER, RICHARD
BONECUTTER, MR. & MRS. JESSE
BRANDSTETTER, REV. A.L. & GRACE
BURSEY, JIM & LOIS
CLARK, MR. & MRS. PAUL
COLLINS, MR. & MRS. DICK
CONKLIN, MILDRED
COX, CORENA
CRAWFORD, EDNA
CREEGER, MR. & MRS. HAROLD
DEAN, MR. & MRS. WARREN
DODSON, IRENE
DUNN, MARYJANE
DUTCHER, MR. & MRS. S.
ECK, MR. & MRS. DAN
ELDER, IRENE
EWERT, REV. WALTER
FEIND, ALICE
GATES, BEULAH
HALE, SCOTT
HAMMOND, MAUDE
HENRY, MILDRED
HILL, FLORENCE
HUNSBERGER, GLADYS
JOHNSON, MR. & MRS. RON

KARODI, SUNDRA
KLIPSCH, MR. & MRS. VERNAL
KNEPPER, MR. & MRS. J.G.
LILLY, LOIS
LUCAS, EDITH
MACK, SELENA
McCLAIN, MR. & MRS. RALPH
McNEAL, DOROTHY
MERKLE, ESTHER
MILLER, DENNIS
MILLER, MR. & MRS. KENNETH
MOUNTAIN, ALMA
PARRISH, MARY
PETERS, JOHN
POST, BERNICE
PRINGLE, GWENETH
PRUETT, ETHEL
PRYOR, ELISABETH
REESE, DORA
RHOADS, MR. & MRS. CHESTER
ROBINSON, HOWARD
RODRIGUEZ, PRISCILLA
SINCLAIR, DEBRA
SNIVELY, MR. & MRS. CECIL
STRIBLING, MILDRED
TATE, LOUISE
TERRY, DR. & MRS. ROBERT
TRENT, MARTHA
TRUMBLE, MARIAN
TUCKER, KAY
TURNELL, ELIZABETH
VOGEL, DOROTHY
WALSH, MR. & MRS. NORMAN
WALTERS, REV. & MRS. DEAN
ZINN, MR. & MRS. CARL

BIBLIOGRAPHY

Anyone seriously contemplating a study of the McCurdy Mission School must first understand the history and the culture of Northern New Mexico. The following books have proven to be especially useful.

Anaya, Rudolfo A. *Bless Me, Ultima.* Berkeley, California: Quinto Sol Publication, 1972.

Bullock, Alice. *Living Legends of the Santa Fe Country.* Santa Fe, New Mexico: Sunstone Press: 1978.

Bullock, Alice. *Mountain Villages,* revised edition. Santa Fe, New Mexico: Sunstone Press, 1982.

Cather, Willa. *Death Comes for the Archbishop.* Vintage Books, 1971.

Chavez, Fray Angelico. *My Penitente Land: Reflection on Spanish New Mexico.* Albuquerque, New Mexico: University of New Mexico Press, 1974.

Henderson , Alice Corbin. *Brothers of Light: The Penitentes of the Southwest.* Santa Fe, New Mexico: William Gannon, 1977.

Hillerman, Tony. *The Spell of New Mexico.* Albuquerque, New Mexico: University of New Mexico Press, 1976.

Horgan, Paul. *Lamy of Santa Fe,* Farrar, Strauss and Giroux, 1975.

LaFarge, Oliver. *Santa Fe.* University of Oklahoma Press, 1959.

Ortiz, Alfonso. *Red Power on the Rio Grande.* Chicago: Follett Publishing Co., 1973.

Otis, Raymond. *Miguel of the Bright Mountain.* Albuquerque: University of New Mexico Press, 1977.

Pack, Arthur N. *We Called it...Ghost Ranch.* Albquiu, New Mexico: Ghost Ranch Conference Center, 1979.

Simmons, Marc. *New Mexico: A History.* W.W. Norton & Co., Inc. 1977.

Sinclair, John. *New Mexico: The Shining Land.* University of New Mexico, 1980.

Weigle, Marta. *Brothers of Light, Brothers of Blood: The Penitentes of the Southwest.* Albuquerque, New Mexico: University of New Mexico Press, 1976.

For the early history and formation of the United Brethren Church in New Mexico:

Minutes of the North Texas Conference 1908–1913. Dayton, Ohio: Microfilm United Seminary.

For a closer examination of the McCurdy Mission School one should examine a number of both published and unpublished sources. Among the more valuable ones are the following:

Bailey, Paul C. *A Biographical Sketch of Mellie Perkins.* Dayton, Ohio: United Theological Seminary, 1960.

Campbell, Rev. Richard C. *Los Conquistadores: The Story of Santa Cruz Church.* Santa Cruz, New Mexico, 1978.

Corbin, Leland Wayne. *The Educational Activities of the E.U.B. Church in New Mexico.* University of New Mexico, 1949.

Gomez, Pedro R., Jr. *a Historical Study of the McCurdy School.* New Mexico Highlands University, 1956.

Maxwell, Dr. Harold H. *The Rocky Mountain Conference History.* Denver, Colorado: Iliff Seminary, 1964.

Megill, Esther L. *Religious Instruction in a Church-Related School: A Study of McCurdy High School, Santa Cruz, New Mexico, With Implications for Curriculum Development.* Hartford, Conn. 1966.

Megill, Harold R. *El Alamo: A Religious History of Santa Cruz, New Mexico.* Tiburon, California: Omega Books 1976.

Morrison, Robert N. *United Brethren Work Among Spanish-American Peoples.* Dayton, Ohio: Bonebrake Theological Seminary, 1942.

Nanninga, Simon P. *The New Mexico School System.* Albuquerque: University of New Mexico Press, 1950.

Wiley, Thomas. *Public School Education in New Mexico.* Albuquerque: University of New Mexico, 1965.

For specific news from McCurdy and other mission schools in New Mexico, one should consult the various church newspapers and magazines.

The Religion Telescope (1834–1946) is especially good on the early years. The *Woman's Evangel* (1882–1917), which became *The Evangel* (1930–1946) in 1930 and which changed its name to *The World Evangel* (1947–1968) contains news from New Mexico in almost every issue. Additionally, several news stories appear in the magazine *Builders,* which was published between 1947 and 1968. Since 1968 news from McCurdy has appeared much less frequently. On occasion stories have appeared in *New World Outlook* and in *Response.*

Readers are referred to the extensive footnotes following each chapter for more information on the McCurdy School and its history.

McCurdy Mission School Oral History Interviews:

Bonecutter, Rev. Maurice. Española, New Mexico, July 11, 1982.
Bonecutter, Mrs. Rhea. Española, New Mexico, July 7, 1982.
Brandstetter, Rev. A.L. Los Alamos, New Mexico, May 14, 1981.
Brewer, Mr. Ronald. Española, New Mexico, July 7, 1982.
Burgett, Mr. David. Española, New Mexico, June 28, 1982
Cole, Miss Irene. Española, New Mexico, July 2, 1982.
Coover, Miss Lois, Española, New Mexico, July 18, 1983.
Eakin, Mrs. Lillian McCurdy, Mechanicsburg, Pennsylvania, April 1, 1982.
Heffner, Rev. Dr. Dennis. Española, New Mexico, June 29, 1982.
Heffner, Mrs. DeeDee. Española, New Mexico. July 2, 1982.
Hilton, Mr. Donald. Española,. New Mexico, June 29, 1982.
Hyde, Mrs. Beth. Española, New Mexico, July 5, 1982.
Hyde, Mr. Will. Española, New Mexico, July 5, 1982.
Lauber, Mr. Larry. Española, New Mexico, June 28, 1982.
McCracken, Mrs. Violet. Santa Fe, New Mexico, May 5 & 8, 1981.
McDonald, Miss Georgene. Española, New Mexico, May 13, 1981.
Marks, Rev. Douglas. Española, New Mexico, July 2, 1982.
Martinez, Mr. Jose M. Antonito, Colorado, May 11, 1981; Española, New
     Mexico, May 22, 1981.
Martinez, Mrs. Marian. Española, New Mexico, July 2, 1981.
Medina, Mrs. Ethel. Española, New Mexico, May 6, 1981.
Muterspaugh, Mrs. Linda. Española, New Mexico, June 29, 1982.
Megill, Mr. & Mrs. Keith. Española, New Mexico, July 12, 1982.
Pringle, Rev. & Mrs. A.W. Española, New Mexico, May 15, 1981.
Pruett, Mrs. Ethel. Española, New Mexico, May 7, 1981.
Robinson, Dr. Dale. Española, New Mexico, May 15, 1981.
Robinson, Mrs. Margaret. Española, New Mexico, July 7, 1982.
Rodriguez, Mr. Enoch. Española, New Mexico, June 30, 1982.
Sanchez, Mr. Ernesto. Española, New Mexico, June 29, 1982.
Sass, Mrs. Joyce. Española, New Mexico, June 28, 1982.
Stambach, Miss Ruth. Española, New Mexico, May 13, 1981.
Townsend, Miss Elvira. Española, New Mexico, June 30, 1982.
Trujillo, Mrs. Max. Vallecitos, New Mexico, June 30, 1983.
Van Essen, Mr. Erwin. Española, New Mexico, July 1, 1982.
Wickersham, Mrs. Marge. Española, New Mexico, July 7, 1982.
Williams, Miss Avis. Española, New Mexico, May 11, 1981.
Zeigler, Dr. Samuel. Española, New Mexico, July 8, 1982.

INDEX

Adult evening school, 106
Advisory Council, 56
Agricultural program, 85-86, 104
Akes, Dr. Leonard, 92, 105
Albuquerque Academy, 20
Alcalde, NM, 20, 34-35, 47,
    54, 56-57, 64, 81-82,
    84-85, 88, 96, 120, 122-123
Alire, Dr. Richard, 109
Allen, Mr. & Mrs. W.A., 61
Allison-James School, 20, 32, 49
Amador, Albert, 62, 83
Amador family, 62-63
Amigos del Valle, 111
Amistad, NM, 25, 27, 29, 56
Ancones, NM, 94
Angel Fire Ski Resort, 121
Archuleta, Father, 114

Bachman Hall, 88
Bachman, Irene, 87-88
Ball, Helen, 95
Bathke, LaVerta, 106, 123
Beringer, Ada, 106
Blake Hall, 45, 105, 112
Blake, Lena, 55-56, 62, 64, 87
Block, John, 53
Board of Trustees, 108-09
Bond & Nohl Co., 91
Bonecutter, Maurice & Rhea, 106
Borrego building, 30
Brandstetter, Rev. Albert L., 26,
    89-90, 94
Brandstetter, Rev. George, 26
Brasher, G.K. ("Bud"), 109
Brawner, Mary, 31-33, 36, 42,
    47, 55-56
Brookhart, Nell, 121
Brooks, Sarah, 56, 64
Brown, Rev. Lewis, 93
Burgett, Carol, 106, 109, 127
Burgett, David S., 106, 127
Bustos family, 42, 45

Caldwell, Evalina, 64
Caldwell, I.E., 64, 95
Camp, Dr. P.M., 36, 45-46

Campbell, Pat (Ashby), 123
Campbell, Rev. Richard, 34, 37,
    45, 53, 93-94, 111, 114
Cañon, NM, 94
Carleton, Bishop Alsie, 113
Carouthers, Ed, 124
Carpenter, Rev. Roy, 95
Cemetery, Alcalde, NM. *See:*
    La Loma Vista Cemetery
Chamita, NM, 95
Cimino, Don, 112
Clapham, NM, 25
Clark, Mr., 34
Clark, Mrs. Jess, 61
Clausius, Ruth, 106, 123
Clinic, 91
Clippinger, Bishop A.R., 83
Clippinger, Lula, 35, 47, 54, 56,
    62-63, 90, 94, 121
Cole, Irene, 95, 103, 106
Colorado United Brethren
    Conference, 61
Cone, NM, 29
Coover, Lois, 92
Cordova, Ercilia, 87
Counseling Service of Northern
    New Mexico, 111
Coupon and stamp projects,
    117-118
Cruz, Victoria, 51

Decker, Rev. Roger, 111
Dixon Case, 81-82, 122
Dormitories, 42, 47, 53, 87,
    112-113 *See also:* names of
    individual dormitories
Dumas, TX, 26
Dye, Rev. & Mrs. W.E., 41, 45

East Ohio Conference, 56
Edith McCurdy Literary Society,
    50
El Rito, NM, 95
Electricity installed, 41
Engle, Mrs. J.R., 91
Enrollment, 30, 36, 41, 43, 47, 64,
    81-82, 95, 105, 113, 122, 126
Española, NM, 15
Española, NM church, 50, 53,
    56-57, 90, 93

Española, NM hospital, 91-92,
    107
Española Valley, 16-17, 29
Española Valley Communities
    Activities (EVCA), 111-112
Española Valley Group
    Ministry, 111, 123
Eva, OK, 26, 29
Evangelical United Brethren
    Summer Service Project, 96
Evans, Mr., 49

First, Peggy, 106
First, Robert ("Bob"), 106, 127
Floris, OK, 25, 29
Flu epidemic (1919), 42
Fogal, Mary Jane, 107, 114
Freshly, Eleanor, 64
Funeral, first at mission, 41

Garcia, Sister Bernice, 114
Garcia, Rafaelita, 28
Garcia, Susana, 56
Garrett, Lula, 124
Gaston, Charity Ann, 20
Gish, Rev. & Mrs. C.C., 56-57
Graduates in 1922, 50
Graduates in 1926, 54
Gregory, Bishop D.T., 93
Griggs, Dr. Zonora, 35
Gutierrez, Fidel, 33
Gymnasium
    Dedication of, 84
    Fire, 83
    Joint use of, 84
    Rebuilding of, 83

Haffner, Bessie, 30, 35
Hague, Virgil, 109
Hamaker, Gertrude E., 61, 63
Hardy, Anna, 35, 55
Hartville, OK, 26
Harwood Industrial School, 20
Harwood, Rev. Thomas, 20
Harwood, Mrs. Thomas, 34
Hastings, Ruth, 107
Hauser Chapel, 31, 36, 56
Hauser, Mr. & Mrs. Richard, 27
Heffner, Rev. Dennis, 111
Hernandez, NM, 93

Herrick, Delia, 56, 62-63, 81, 96
Herrick House, 87
Herrick, Lowell P., 61, 96
Herrick, Vera, 61, 96
Herrick, Zella, 61, 86, 96
Hillis, Rev. Robert, 25
Hilton, Don & Mary, 106
Hollenhead, Sam, 112
Holy Cross Church & School,
    Santa Cruz, NM, 113-114
Homestead Act of 1862, 25
Houser, Richard, Sr., 89
Hovermale Memorial
    Elementary School, 96
Hovermale, U.P., 89, 93, 96
Howe, Joseph G., 61
Huffman, Rev. Nicholas, 29-30
Hunsberger, Gerald, 106, 116
Hunsberger, Marcia, 106

Jacquez, Eloy & Rosina, 106
Jaramillo, Florence, 109
John Hyson Presbyterian School,
    Chimayo, NM, 114
Jordon, Rev. & Mrs. Andy, 93

Kendig, Lillian, 31-32, 34, 36-37,
    41, 45-47, 50, 52, 125
Kephart, Bishop, 30, 48
King, Rev. Mrs. Callie, 25, 27,
    36, 41
La Loma Vista Cemetery, 42,
    54, 123
La Madera, NM, 95
Land purchases, 109-111
Langdon, Marie, 64, 81, 88
Las Vegas, NM, 26
Lauber, Larry & Sharon, 106
Lipscomb, TX, 26
Lobb, Rev. & Mrs. Walter, 84
Loretto Academy, Santa Fe,
    NM, 20, 49
Los Alamos, NM 89-90, 123
Lucero, Richard, 113
Luckey, Leila, 32, 35
Luna, J.R., 56

McCracken, Glen F., 56-63, 81-
    86, 88-90, 96-98, 103-105,
    109, 114-115, 123, 126

McCracken, Violet
    (Mrs. Glen F.), 84, 97
McCurdy Chapel, 84, 93
McCurdy, Edith, 27, 30-31, 46
McCurdy, Mr. & Mrs. E.E., 36
McCurdy Road, 30
McDonald, Georgene, 81, 88,
    120, 122
McFarland, Paul, 92
Markey, Lillian, 32-33
Martin, Barbara, 92
Martinez Field, 117
Martinez, José Manuel ("Chic"),
    44, 51, 54, 116-117
Martinez, Manuel, 50
Martinez, Manuelita, 36, 44
Martinez, Susanita, 28, 32
Matzigkeit, Everett, 127
Medina, Candido, 51, 54, 62,
    64, 93, 96
Medina, Mrs. Ethel, 64, 96
Megill, Esther, 119
Megill, Rev. Harold, 56
Megill, Pearl (Mrs. Harold), 56
Megill, Keith, 112
Menaul School, Albuquerque,
    NM, 50
Middlewater, TX, 25
Miller, Ralph, 106
Mission buildings, 28, 30, 36, 47
Moffat, Lillian, 91-92
Moore, Irma, 31, 35
Mosher, Bruce C., 114
Munns, Violet, 61
Muterspaugh, Lloyd & Linda,
    106, 127

New Mexico
    Admitted to Union, 18
    American occupation of, 20
    Civil War in, 18
    Conquistadores, 14
    Education in, 19-22
    Geography of, 13
    Mexican province, a, 17
    Mining, 18
    Mission schools, 20
    Pre-Columbian, 14
    Prehistoric, 14
    Pueblo Revolt, 16

New Mexico, continued
    Railroads, 18
    Spanish settlers, 14-17
    U.S. territory, as a, 17-18
New Mexico Conference, 29,
    52, 61, 113
Newman, Cora, 56, 62, 64
Newman, Lottie, 36, 41
Nichols, Rev. Maurice, 56, 61,
    63, 83
Nicholson, Rev. E.G., 20
Norris, Jane, 64
North Texas Conference, 25-27,
    29, 33, 36-37
Northern New Mexico Com-
    munity College, 106, 108

Odell, Roger, 106
Olsen, Mr., 63
Onava, NM, 29
Opposition to McCurdy
    Mission School, 32-33, 43-44,
    51, 53, 55, 82-83, 109
Optima, OK, 25, 29
Outreach services, 45, 51, 95,
    106-107, 111-112, 120-122
Overmiller, Rev. John, 41,
    46-57, 61, 85, 96, 125
Overmiller, Mrs. John, 47, 50
Overmiller, Vonda Mae, 50

Pack, Arthur, 85, 91-92
Pack, Mrs. Arthur, 91
Peabody, Mr., 92
Perkins, Mellie, 26-37, 52-53,
    55, 64, 120, 122
Petaca, NM, 84, 95
Peterson, Charles, 41, 46
Peterson, Mrs. Charles, 46
Peterson, Esther, 36
Plumbing installed, 41
Post, Bernice, 112
Presbyterian Hospital,
    Embudo, NM, 55
Pringle, Rev. Adolphus ('Dolph'),
    94-95, 103, 114, 121
Pringle, Gwen (Mrs. Adolphus),
    94-95, 121

Rasor, Freda, 54

Religious Life Committee, 119
Richter, Rev. & Mrs. George, 84
Rinconada, NM, 20
Rio Grande Industrial School, 20
Robinson, Dale E., 103-106, 108, 111, 114, 117, 126
Robinson, Margaret (Mrs. Dale E.), 103-104
Rodriguez, Enoch, 106, 115, 117
Rodriguez, Eustie (Mrs. Enoch), 106
Romero, Angelica, 30
Romero, Helica, 36
Roybal, Fidel, 36

St. Michael's College, Santa Fe, NM, 20
Salaries, 47, 88-89, 105, 122, 126
Salazar, Rev. T.Z., 33-34
San Ildefonso Pueblo, 30
San Juan Pueblo, 15-16
Sanchez, Ernest, 106, 113
Sanchez, Rev. Harold, 93
Sanchez, Margie, 106
Santa Cruz, 30-34, 36, 41, 47-48, 50, 53, 55-57, 61-62, 82, 84-85, 90, 93-96, 121
Santa Fe, NM, 29
Sass, Joyce, 106
Schafer, Anna A., 90-91
Scheaffer, Eleanor, 64
Schlotterbeck, Rev. Clarence, 25-27, 30, 84
School of Practical Nursing, 106-108
Sedan, NM, 26, 29, 56
Shanklin, Ella, 35
Shockey, Sally, 116
Short, Carrie, 42
Smith, Betty, 117
Smith, Nancy, 61
Smith, Ruth, 41, 45, 47, 52
Spanish Prayer Group, 84-85
Specht, Ruth, 92
Sports, 49-50, 112, 115-117, 122
Stambach, Ruth Marie, 106, 119
Statton, Bishop, 63
Student Center, new, 112-113

Taos, NM, 19
Taylor, Lawrence, 90
Templeton, Rev. & Mrs. Richard, 94
Testermann, Pearl.
    See Megill, Pearl
Thompson, James, 109
Townsend, Elvira, 106
Tres Piedras, NM, 84, 121
Trujillo, Max, 94, 121
Tuition, 43, 47, 50, 88, 105, 122

United Brethren, 25, 50, 53, 56
United Methodist Church, 108, 124-125

Valdez, Ralph, 93
Vallecitos, NM, 35, 62-64, 85, 90, 94-96, 120-121, 123
Van Essen, Erwin, 115
Velarde, NM, 27-35, 41-42, 47, 50, 55-57, 62, 64, 81, 84, 85, 87, 96, 120, 122-123
Vermillion, Lillian, 95
Vesqa, Father Mario, 114
Vialpando, Robert, 54
Vogel, Dorothy, 92

Wagon Mound, NM, 26, 29, 33, 121
Wannamaker, Rev., 25
Warren, Florence, 54, 62
Watrous, NM, 20
Wedding, first at mission, 41
Werkley, Bishop William, 25
White, Myrtle, 56
Whitney, Dr. C., 29
Wiggen Memorial United Brethren Church, Vallecitos, NM, 63
Wilhide, Bessie, 45
Willard, Frank, 91
Williams, Arthur, 63
Williams, Avis, 82, 106, 122-123
Willow Creek, NM, 26
Wolford, Pearl, 81
Wolheiter, Bertha, 35, 41-42, 47, 54
Womelsduff, John, 41

World War II, 89
Wrye, Whrelda, 61

Young, Rev. & Mrs. William, 92
York College, York, NE, 54, 57, 61, 84, 96
York, Rev. & Mrs. Wilbur, 84

Zeigler, Dr. Samuel G., 91-92

ABOUT THE AUTHOR

Dr. Robert H. Terry, a native Pennsylvanian, is a professor of history at York College of Pennsylvania and director of its Oral History Center. An active member of Calvary United Methodist Church in Dillsburg, Pennsylvania, Bob began delving into the history of the McCurdy Mission School during 1980 when he did volunteer work along with his wife, Shirley, at the mission in Española, New Mexico. The results of his endeavors unfold in the pages of *Light In The Valley*.

Dr. Terry has published a number of other books, monographs and articles. In addition to teaching and writing, Bob participates in a variety of church and community activities. He is a Lay Speaker, Conference, and Jurisdictional delegate of the United Methodist Church.